ARISTOTLE

N. JAYAPALAN

ATLANTIC PUBLISHERS AND DISTRIBUTORS

Published by
ATLANTIC PUBLISHERS AND DISTRIBUTORS
B-2, Vishal Enclave, Opp. Rajouri Garden, New Delhi-27
Phones : 5413460, 5429987

Sales Office
4215/1, Ansari Road, Darya Ganj, New Delhi-110 002
Phones : 3273880, 3285873, 3280451
Fax : 91-11-3285873
e-mail : gupta.atlantc@axcess.net.in

Typeset at
APD Computer Graphics, Delhi

Printed in India at
Mehra Offset Press, Delhi

Preface

It gives me great pleasure to place this book in the hands of the readers. I am fully aware of the fact that there is a good number of excellent books on Aristotle and the history of Western political thought written by eminent English and American Scholars but they do not meet the requirements of the Indian students. So, in order to facilitate the task of the students of Indian universities and to enable the layman to have an understanding and knowledge of many political ideas I have written this book.

In writing this book I do not claim any originality but at the same time my own political training has enabled me to give my own interpretation of events and facts on many issues. I have tried my best to maintain an impartial attitude in the exposition of various doctrines. My aim has been throughout to give students and laymen an easily intelligible exposition of various political ideas and institutions of Aristotle.

The subject has been dealt with in a very simple and lucid language. I take this opportunity of acknowledging my top indebtedness to various great and eminent scholars and teachers of Political Science from whose works I have borrowed freely and profusely.

I am thankful to the M/s Atlantic Publishers and Distributors, New Delhi for readily agreeing to publish this book and bringing it expeditiously and efficiently.

Suggestions, if any, for the improvement of the book are always welcomed and shall be gratefully acknowledged in the next edition.

N. JAYAPALAN

Contents

1

Aristotle — His Life and Times

If the world is indebted to Plato for idealism in politics, it is indebted to Aristotle for realism in thought and action. Aristotle has been "the philosopher" of the ages. He has been rightly called "The Master of those who know." No wonder he serves as a connecting link between the Orient and the Occident. He was in fact, the master of every branch of existing knowledge except mathematics. Founder of the science of logic, he wrote on theology, metaphysics, ethics, economics, aesthetics and physics. His 'Politics' is a classical statement of Greek political thought.

Aristotle was born in 384 B.C. at Stagira in the Thracian Peninsula. His father Nichomachus was a physician to Philip, the king of Macedonia. He lived in Macedonia for many years. His youth was spent abroad. He was left an orphan and was brought up under the guardianship of the friends of his family in Mycia. Since his childhood was spent in Macedonian court, where the surroundings were of scientific culture, he imbibed interest in physical science and the disposition to view things from the standpoint of a biologist.

At the age of 17, Aristotle joined Plato's Academy at Athens and sat at the feet of his master, Plato for 20 years from 367 to 347 B.C. It is during this period that Aristotle's philosophy took shape. In 347 B.C. on Plato's death, Aristotle left Athens for 13 years. During this period he first stayed at Atarneves at the court of Hermias for sometime. There he served as court physician. For about 3 years, he was invited to Philip's court as Alexander's tutor (346-343 B.C.). He remained there till Alexander was 16. Alexander did not fully take to heart the master's teaching, but he reposed confidence in Greeks as asked by his master and gave them sufficient liberty. Then he returned to Athens and stayed there for about 12 years when practically all his surviving books were written.

Aristotle married the adopted daughter of his friend, the tyrant Hermias. This marriage was successful and accounts for his devotion to the institution of the family and his opposition to Plato's communism of wives. He was a man of comfortable life and believed in the necessity of private property.

Aristotle's time was one of the most troubled in the history of Greece.

There was lawless democracy or selfish oligarchy obtaining in most of the Hellenic city-states. But the Macedonians were not deemed to be true Hellens as they were governed by kings and did not live in city-states. After Alexander's death, Aristotle was, for a short time in trouble. His enemies preferred an indictment against him. Charging him with irreligion and doing homage to the dynast Hermias. Aristotle took to flight, for "Athens must not sin a second time against philosophy." He returned to his estate in Chalcies and died in 322 B.C. in Enboea at the comparatively early age of 62.

Inspite of his active contact with Alexander, and his empire, Aristotle conceived of things in terms of Hellas and the city-state. Nature, to Aristotle, had meant the Greek to be the superior and the barbarian the inferior being. Non-Greek institutions and politics, therefore, did not interest Aristotle.

Aristotle started his school, the Lyceum, in Athens in 335 B.C. which became the intellectual centre of Hellas in his days and after. The versatile genius and great systematiser of human knowledge attracted pupils from far and wide. He founded new branches of knowledge and created sciences "so widely divergent as logic and comparative astronomy." During this period he wrote most of his books. The study of them was revived by Andronicus of Rhodes in time of Cicero.

Aristotle's political philosophy reflects three main influences. His thought was, firstly, affected by the decline of the city-state in his days. Again he was deeply affected by the current Hellenic prejudices and beliefs such as the essential superiority of the Greek over the non-Greek and the city-state over other forms of social organisation, active role of the citizen in public life, priority of the state over the individual and usefulness of slavery. The third major influence on Aristotle was Plato.

Aristotle's Indebtedness to Plato

There is a considerable indebtedness of Aristotle to Plato in spite of his many criticisms. There is a considerable similarity of ideals in the Laws of Plato and the Politics of Aristotle. Both hold that man is a social animal and must live in society. Both write on the basis of the city-state. Both are for the individual placing himself at the service of the society. There is good deal of similarity in the views of the two about education and educational systems. Both favour state regulation of education. Both have an exalted notion of citizenship and its duties. Both disregard lower classes. Neither denounces slavery.

Plato and Aristotle portray an ideal state. Both insist on unity and harmony of the state. Both denounce democracy and assign rule to virtue. Both take an organic view of society. Both believe in a mixed constitution as the most excellent. To both, justice lies in the rendering of the 'due'. Both believe that the state exists not only for life but good life. Both correlate Ethics and Politics. To Plato, the Ideal is prior to the Actual, to Aristotle, the end is prior to Being. Reality lies in the ideal end of a thing.

According to Maxey, countless admirers have acclaimed Aristotle as 'The Master of them that know', and have ascribed to him the most profound and encyclopaedic mind of all antiquity. The fact remains that few men have spoken authoritatively on so many different subjects, and none perhaps, have even approached the solitary eminence of the stagirite as a court of final appeal in things intellectual. For centuries Aristotle on Logic, Aristotle on Mechanics, Aristotle on Physics, Aristotle on Physiology, Aristotle on Astronomy, Aristotle on Metaphysics, Aristotle on Ethics, Aristotle on Art, Aristotle on Poetry, Aristotle on Economics and Aristotle on Politics, was almost the last word — the unimpeachable authority then which none was more authentic. His information was so much vaster and more exhaustive, his insight so much more penetrating, his deductions so much more plausible than was true of any of his contemporaries or any of his successors prior to the advent of modern science that he became the all-knowing master in whom the scholastic mind could find no fault.

The political atmosphere in which Aristotle lived was not quite different from that of Plato. He too, like Plato, lived through anarchy and war in the Greek city-states. During his life he had witnessed the most important and most disastrous periods of Greek history. The battle of Chaeronea had been fought in 338 B.C. and in it the entire Greek world lost its independence. The glory of city-states had gone. Aristotle himself laments the great degeneration of the times. Unity under these conditions seemed an impossibility. So, like Plato, for Aristotle, unity and stability of Greek life became a watchword. Thus, his preliminary political studies were highly influenced by the political atmosphere in which he happened to live. According to McIlwain, "His preliminary studies include a collection and summary statement of the political changes that had occurred, and of the political conditions which actually existed in more than one hundred and fifty of the separate little city-states about the Aegean and beyond." He found that the disunity was the main reason for the instability of the city-states. The peace that was forced on Athens by the Macedonian rulers proved to be a great blessing for Aristotle. "It permitted Aristotle to organise a course of studies and to initiate a vast scheme of research into the history of political organisations, of science and philosophy — the study of the constitutions of Greek States, of the history of mathematics and medicine, and of the opinion of philosophers as well as into the natural history of minerals, plants and animals and to lay the foundation thereby for one of the first attempts at an encyclopaedia organisation of human knowledge." In this way Richard Mckeon expresses his views about Aristotle in his book "Introduction to Aristotle."

Aristotle — A Genius

Aristotle was a versatile genius. Plato recognises the greatness of his pupil by describing him as the Nous of the Academy — intelligence personified. His genius has come to be recognised universally. If Dante describes him as "The master of them that know", Professor Catlin calls him "the greatest of the encyclopaedists of learning — and the first." He is commonly called the father of political science. He had knowledge of almost all subjects, excepting perhaps mathematics. Thought he wrote a large number of books and treatises on all subjects, most of his works have been lost. Those which have been recovered disclose a mind of prodigious erudition and amazing versatility.

According to Coker, "The range of his discussion is comprehensive, his analysis is systematic; his exposition is thorough and fully illustrated from his relatively wide historical knowledge and extensive observation of contemporary governments."

"There is probably no parallel in the history of mankind either to the vastness of his intellectual achievement or the extent of its subsequent influence" says Foster in his 'Masters of Political Thought'.

Of the various products of his pen, there is a record of six treatises on various phases of logic, twenty-six on different subjects in the field of natural sciences, four on ethics and morals, three on art and poetry, one each on metaphysics, economics, history and politics and four or more on miscellaneous subjects. He was indeed a great genius, who had no parallel in the history of mankind.

2

Aristotle — His Style and Method

The writings of Aristotle are not easy to follow. They are tainted with many faults. "Amongst them are extreme contentiousness about small points; his lack of arrangement, his habit of repeating himself but each time with small differences, which make a wonder whether he means to say something different or has merely forgotten what he said before, the grudging acknowledgement of his debt to his masters and predecessors, especially Plato, the seeming wilfulness of his misunderstanding in certain of the criticisms of them, his crabbed style, his pedagogic manner."

Aristotle's books are full of irrelevant cross-references, back references and of promises, unredeemed, of later discussions. Most of these defects may be due to the fact that his books have come down to us as notes for lectures or notes of his students from his lectures rather than finished products.

The method used by Aristotle for his investigations was scientific. In other words, his method of treatment of a subject is, to a large extent, inductive, aporetic, analytical and dialectic. Though the scientific method was in use before him also, according to Mckeon, "Its novelties centre about the treatment of causes, by which the application of principles to things is insured, and the analysis of terms and propositions, by which the accuracy of statement and interference is ascertained." Aristotle is analytical and logical in his treatment of his subject. He gives up one *a priori* method of deducting ideas from abstract notions of virtue and good followed by Plato and uses the inductive method of formulating his theories as a result of extensive observation and minute analysis of objective facts.

Aristotle was practical and realist. It was his realism with its hard logic, fine analysis, keen observation and a touch of idealism that made him philosopher and scientist of all ages, and his philosophy, a philosophy of universal interest.

Aristotle's material formulation of his theories is in the form of existing customs, institutions and material. This made him conservative in outlook. It makes him attach even Plato's philosophy of one Ideal State and what it contained, communism and education philosopher-ruler, etc. He opposes the Root and Branch methods of Plato's communism. His conservatism of course, is not reactionary; it is progressive. He is a liberal democrat who is opposed to class-rule. He follows the golden mean. This is like pure, progressive conservatism of today.

Aristotle classifies sciences into three groups, *viz.*, (1) Theoretical Sciences, (2) Poetical Sciences and (3) Practical Sciences. *Theoretical Sciences i.e.*, metaphysics, mathematics and physics which deal with material unalterable by man and, therefore, seek the truth.

Poetical Sciences, *i.e.*, poetry, rhetoric and medicine.

Practical Sciences deal with alterable objects.

According to Aristotle there is no clear line of demarcation between ethics and politics; yet he distinguished between the two more than did Plato in whose hands politics was swallowed up by ethics. To him Politics includes *ethics*, the science of individual good, *economics*, the science of family good and *politics*, the science of the good of the social whole. Aristotle, like Plato, assigned moral and spiritual values to associated life in the state, though he disagreed with Plato's idealism. He agreed with Plato that the life of virtue, was the end of both, *i.e.*, of the individual and the state, and therefore, of both ethics and politics.

It goes without saying that real political science in the West begins, not with Plato, but with Aristotle, who laid the foundations of the subject with rare political insight and systematic treatment. Some of the political observations and theories of Aristotle are very shrewd, apply to all forms of social and political life and so the universal and permanent in Aristotle. His political sanity makes him a safe guide for future generations. He puts up an exalted civic ideal of a State Government by reason and law. All free-born are allowed some participation in civic affairs. The end of the State is not merely life but virtuous and happy life. The writings of Aristotle have reference to the Hellenic city-state and ignore other forms of government of non-Hellenic forms of social and economic organisation.

Like a true scientist, Aristotle had the art of distinguishing between the essential and the non-essential and between categories. Whereas with Plato, Politics was a handmade of Ethics, Aristotle separated the two and treated them systematically in two different treatises, *i.e.*, his Politics and the Nichomachean Ethics. Plato viewed society dynamically; Aristotle looked at society statically; Plato lost in the mysticism of the universal, the Eternal and the Absolute; Aristotle worked on society empirically. The scientific nature of the political observation and speculations of Aristotle is thus evident from his empirical study of the existing material but also from his method of approach to the subject. His classification of constitutions and the treatment of the morphology and pathology of the state are clear evidences for his scientific nature of the political observation and speculation.

Thus, Aristotle's style and method is unique and everlasting in the history of political science.

3

The Influence of Plato Over Aristotle

The Influence of Plato over Aristotle cannot be minimised or under estimated. It is tremendous as well as wonderful.

"There is no doubt that Aristotle never misses an opportunity to criticise his master, and is more conscious of his differences than of the points of agreement with him." But these differences should not blind us to discern the indebtedness of Aristotle to Plato. It is true that his keen intellect did not allow him to be blind follower of Plato and accept what the master taught him. But he made the master's teachings the basis of his own thinking and developed them along the lines determined by his earlier biological studies and scientific temperament.

According to Will Durant, Aristotle says, 'Dear is Plato but dearer still is truth." We agree with Foster that Aristotle is the greatest of all Platonists, that he is "permeated by Platonism to a degree in which perhaps no great philosopher, besides him, has been permeated by the thought of another".

Wayper says, "Inspite of Aristotle's criticisms, usually niggling though occasionally trenchant, of Plato, the difference between them is more formal than real." C.E.M. Joad is of the same view when he says, "Aristotle has a habit of starting and starting avowedly from positions which are anti-thesis of those of Plato, yet ending in conclusions which are scarcely if at all distinguishable from those of his predecessor".

Dunning makes Aristotle's relation with Plato clearer, "He differs from his master Plato, much more in the form and method than in the substance of his thought. Most of the ideas which seem characteristically Aristotelian are to be found in Plato. But the Platonic expression of them is generally in the form of a suggestion or allusion or illustration; while in Aristotle they appear as definite, clear-cut dogmas, bearing an unmistakable relation to the general system of scientific doctrine. This contrast is rooted in the respective intellectual peculiarities of the philosophers".

It is not the least surprising that Aristotle may have great similarity with Plato. It is because of the fact that he remained disciple of Plato for 20 years at the latter's Academy. He was to head the Academy after Plato's death but Spensippus became its director and he could not succeed. According to Salime, "Every page of his (Aristotle's) later philosophical writings bears witness to this connection". Both Plato and Aristotle commonly inherited the legacies of Homer to Socrates. In the words of Foster, "Both of them looked with alarm on the instability of Greek political life and on the moral anarchy which they believed that the antidote lay in education for a better way of living. Both believed that the good life could only be lived in a city-state of moderate size, could not be attained by all men, but only by those who had sufficient means and schooling to do so. Both, therefore, wished to limit citizenship so as to make this possible, and both thought it right that manual labour should be done by slaves or by non-citizens".

Aristotle's political ideal was quite at one with Plato's in setting up an ethical purpose as the chief end of the State. The real purpose of a State ought to include the moral improvement of its citizens, because it ought to be an association of men living together to achieve the best possible life. This is the idea of meaning of a State. The State alone is self-sufficing in the sense that it alone provided all the conditions within which the highest type of moral development can take place.

More points of similarity between the two philosophers are that Aristotle, like Plato is conservative as he also confines his ideal to the city-state as the basis of his political thought. Both are Athenians but under the influence of Sparta and they protect oligarchical character of society. Both are of the view that education should begin when a child is conceived. Both lay stress on check of population by birth control and destruction of unhealthy children. Both are metaphysical in so far as they say that nature has made some men of gold, silver and copper. They regard the State as a moral and spiritual entity as they believe that 'Good' is the ultimate end of the State although in the case of Plato, it is absolute and in the case of Aristotle, it is relative. They hold that Ethics constitute a single and indivisible science. Their political thought is ethical in character. They believe that the only life which is worthy of man is a life of virtue and that it is made possible for an individual in and through membership of the State. Aristotle agrees with Plato against the Sophists that the State comes into being for the sake of life and continues for the sake of good life. Both the philosophers aim at unity, but their methods differ; they equate State and Society and give no right to man against the State. Both are against trade and industry and usury. In taking all knowledge to be his province Aristotle was a true child of the Academy.

There is not much difference between the two philosophers for the reason that Plato was firm to his ideal to the end, but Aristotle was after ideals which he borrowed from Plato but modified as and when tested according to practical experience. That is why Plato is known as idealist and Aristotle as a realist.

All the same, according to Barker, Aristotle borrowed many points to extent of verbal copying. He gives equal importance to women as Plato did. He attracts Plato's ideal State and not his sub-ideal State. That is why Aristotle's ideal State is considered Plato's second best State.

When we examine the place occupied by education in the writings of these two, we find that they are almost equal. In fact. "Aristotle was genuine Platonist in so far as he believes that the greatest need of the times was the proper education of the rulers". In the case of Plato, education is the instrument thought which the ideal State can be realised. In the case of Aristotle, even though it is not the medium, it occupies a prominent place in his Best Average State. As a matter of fact, he discusses at length about the place and importance of education in his Best Practicable State. Unfortunately, it was not carried to its logical conclusion. It may be due to his death.

In constructing his Ideal State he draws considerably on the Laws of Plato. Plato in his Laws has stated that when men are without laws they differ not at all from the most savage beast. Aristotle says "Man, when perfected in the best of animals, but when separated from law and justice he is worst of all." This is almost verbal copying. Plato said that as it was not possible to procure philosopher-guardians, law must be made sovereign. Aristotle also made the law sovereign in his State. Again Aristotle borrowed the origin of State from Plato as stated in the Laws that first there were isolated families, then villages, and then came the State. The requirements of his Ideal State, like the specifications regarding population, its character, size, situation and nature are derived from the Laws. It is true that his Ideal State differs greatly from the Ideal State of the Republic but resembles a good deal the sub-Ideal State of Laws.

In other words, Aristotle's Best is Plato's Second Best, Aristotle's remarks while introducing the best State are inspired by Plato's discussion on the physical, economic and social factors which govern the nature of State.

Plato argues at places that excess is dangerous and Aristotle is considered one of the greatest experiments of the golden mean in politics. For both, Plato and Aristotle man is a political animal and can only fulfil himself in the State. The Classification of the State of Aristotle is almost similar to that of Plato because the names of the classified States are the same even though the methods are different. For both the State and the individual are complementary but not contradictory. In both there is a king of aristocratic temper, Plato with his philosopher guardians and Aristotle with his limited citizenship.

In the words of G. Grote, "the organisation of government proposed by Aristotle in the two last Books of his Politics, as representing his own ideas of something like perfection is evidently founded upon the Republic of Plato, from whom he differs in the important circumstances of not admitting either community of property or community of wives and children. Each of these philosophers recognises one separate class of inhabitants, relieved from all private toil and all money, getting employment, and constituting exclusively the citizens of the commonwealth. This small class is in fact the city — the commonwealth; the remaining inhabitants, are not a part of commonwealth, they are only appendages to it — indispensable indeed, but still appendages in the same manner as slaves are kept." Grote recognises that Aristotle's Best State, where deviates from the Republic, largely copies Plato's Laws.

Aristotle's thought is entirely dominated by Plato's. Somewhat grudgingly he followed his great teacher as closely as his temperament permitted. So he endorsed and systematised Plato's rationalistic theory of slaves. In some minor points Aristotle slightly mitigates Plato's theory of slavery and duly censors his teacher for being too harsh.

Aristotle's Best State is a compromise between three things : a romantic Platonic aristocracy; a sound and balanced feudalism and some democratic ideas but feudalism was the best of it. With the democrats Aristotle needs that all citizens should have the right to participate in the government. But, this of course, is not meant to be as radical as it sounds, for Aristotle, explains at once that not only slaves but all members of the producing classes are excluded from citizenship. Thus, he teaches with Plato that the working class must not rule and the ruling class must not produce. It is in the same vein that he repeatedly insists that "the first principle of all action is leisure."

It is said that Aristotle made a profession of Platonic philosophy. He only systematised Platonism. Zeller says that Aristotle "can inspire us in the same way as Plato does. His work is direct, more professional than plato's has been." It is quite true to say that "in fundamental of his political philosophy, Aristotle was a faithful disciple of Plato". To conclude in the language of C.E.M. Joad, "In the end he (Aristotle) is found to have done little more that dot the i's and cross the t's of the propositions already reached by Plato."

4

Aristotle — The Father of Political Science

Aristotle is often remembered as the Father of Political Science. It is due to his great contributions to Political Thought of the world. The political philosophy of Aristotle is empirical and descriptive in comparison with the radical and abstract nature of Plato's philosophy. Inspite of many repetitions and certain inconsistencies the central theme of his 'Politics', is balance or moderation. Hence, the remark of Catlin that "after Confucius, Aristotle is the supreme apostle of commonsense and the Golden mean." Moreover, the confusion or digressions of Aristotle are responsible for opening new chapters in Political Science. The main theme of Aristotle is to reconcile ideals and actualities. In doing so he dealt with most of our modern problems. No doubt, he deviated a long way from Plato, but we are fortunate for the very reason as that made him widen the scope of Political Science.

Aristotle's theories are based on a detailed knowledge of the past history and on a reliance on the teachings of experience in history. He condemns Plato for paying insufficient attention to history and creating schemes of Government without due reference either to the nature of human, animal or actual form of government. According to Salime, the true romance of the Republic is the romance of a free intelligence, unbound by custom and untrammelled by facts. But Aristotle had a great love for facts because of his biological training and scientific studies, which made him a careful and systematic observer.

Aristotle had an extraordinary knowledge of the political institutions both of his own times and of the past. It is said that he had studied over 150 constitutions before he wrote his 'Politics'. Political studies thus became empirical or inductive to his hands. He may, therefore, legitimately be considered the father of the study of comparative government.

This new method of first knowing the constitutional history and then arriving at general conclusions is his great achievement. Salime says,

Aristotle is the founder of the historical method which has been on the whole the soundest and the most fruitful that the study of Politics has evolved. In the words of Karl Frederick, "He (Aristotle) was the first man in the world's literature who applied a deeply inductive (experimental or comparative) method to the diverse phenomenon of the State." It is one of his chief contributions to political science.

Besides attaching great importance to collection of facts, he stressed the problem of value and importance of ethical judgements. He judged the significance of the facts in terms of the end or purpose of the State, because Politics was to him, the culmination of Ethics. He was the first realist in his thought as against idealism of Plato. While his teacher roved in the imaginary world of idealism, he dealt with the reforming of actuals. That is why Plato could not be honoured with the title of 'Father of Political Science' which has been bestowed upon him. "It was his great regard for facts which prevented Aristotle from being radical; he could not be anything more than a reformist. A person who attaches great importance to the accumulated wisdom of past cannot become a revolutionary. The whole bent and bias of his mind led Aristotle to believe that in order to be effective an ideal must not go against the actual state of affairs" :

Aristotle never completed his ideal State for which he gave introduction in his Book III. It is because of the reason, these ideals were sunk in the mid stream of realities. Hence, the remark of Salime, "what all he wrote was a book not on an Ideal State, but on the ideals of State". This fact in Aristotle's philosophy is due to the reason that he was more empirical and descriptive. He did not have the bold sweep and courage of Plato to destroy all that stood in his way. He is more cautious and moderate. To put it in other words, he is more of a reformatory than revolutionary. What he did was to bring the ideal of Plato down to earth; and accepting his general view of proportion and harmony adopt it to the practical politics of the city-state. This new line, he took up did not lead to any barren results. This revolt on Plato fruitful in the sense that he opened new world in Political Science.

Maxey puts this difference between Plato and Aristotle in beautiful words, "As Plato is father to the idealists, romanticists, revolutionists and utopians of political philosophy, so Aristotle is father to the realists, scientists, pragmatists and utilitarians. All who believe in new worlds for old are disciples of Plato all who believe in old worlds made new by the tedious and toilsome use of science are disciple of Aristotle". Again, "Where Plato lets his imagination take flight, Aristotle is factual and dull; where Plato is eloquent, Aristotle is exact; where Plato leaps from general concepts to logical conclusions, Aristotle slowly works from multitude of facts; where Plato gives us an ideal commonwealth that is the best his mind can conceive, Aristotle gives us the material requisites out of which, by adopting to the circumstances, a model State can be constructed."

The chief difficulty or defect of Plato's philosophy is that it is cut up into two incompatible halves. His ideal State of 'Republic' has absolute rule of the philosopher-king untrammelled by law or consent of the people. But his second best State of 'The Laws' give importance to laws and public consent. This he does grudgingly and, therefore, he is not able to restore law properly as it required complete revision of the psychology and the theory of knowledge underlying the 'Republic'. Aristotle took up the hint and the direction suggested by Plato and restored law to its proper place, rather he established sovereignty of law in the State. The Laws made him regard law not as to make shift but as an indispensable condition of a moral and civilised life. An introductory passage in the 'Polity' was evidently written with one Plato's remarkable utterances in mind : "Man, when perfected, is the best of animals. But when separated from law and justice, he is worst of all." Aristotle believes that in the making, of law, the collective wisdom of a people is superior to that of even the wisest ruler. He regards supremacy of law as a mark of a good State and not merely as an unfortunate necessity. In the words of Salime, "Even the wise ruler cannot dispense with law because the law has an impersonal quality which no man, however good, can attain." The law is "reason unaffected by desire."

Because of this regard for law, Aristotle laid emphasis on constitutional rule as it is, to him, consistent with the dignity of the subject, whereas a personal or despotic rule is not. The constitutional ruler, according to Aristotle rule over willing subjects. He rules by consent. To Aristotle constitutional rule is the rule in the public interest as against a factional or personal interest; it is lawful rule in the sense that government is carried on by general regulations and not by arbitrary decrees.

Aristotle did not like to confine the scope of political science to the construction of the ideal State as it was for Plato, but he wanted that it should be widened to include a study of the actual States also. According to him, political science should teach the art of governing and organising all types of States, good as well as bad. He himself discusses how even tyrannies may be preserved. While dealing with the actual State he does not use the deductive method of Plato but descriptive or inductive. He defines and describes the features of various forms of Government and gives the causes of their decay and the best ways to preserve them. In dealing with these actualities he divorces politics from ethics and thereby seems to be most modern. The middle portion of his 'Politics' is entirely empirical and moral considerations are put aside. At places his treatment is almost Machiavellian.

It does not mean that he rejects the ethical purpose of the State. He retains these basic ideal derived from Plato, but he goes farther than his master, and in so doing introduces fundamental modifications. Besides the moral end of the State, he includes in his new and more general science of politics, 'an empirical study of elements of State, both political and social, of actual constitutions their combinations; and the consequences which are found to follow from these combinations.' In the words of Salime, according to Aristotle, "the complete art of the statesman must take governments as they are and do the best it can with the means it has. It might even divorce itself from moral considerations altogether and tell the tyrant how to succeed in tyranny." This widening of the definition and conception of political science is Aristotle's profound contribution to the subject.

Aristotle defines a constitution as an arrangement of citizens, or a kind of life, and a form of government is the expression of the kind of life which the State is designed to foster. A change in form of government would signify a change in the constitution or the underlying kind of-life-that citizens are trying to realise. He is shrewd enough to observe that a political constitution is one thing and the way it works is different thing. A Given form of government would work in a very different way if a new social class acquires ascendancy. Aristotle does not fail to notice that the political structure of a State depends upon the social and economic structure of society.

Not only does he recognise the importance of economic in finances but also of geographic conditions on political organisation and activity. Besides, the character of a constitution and its actual working depends upon the way in which the three elements of the State — deliberative, Judicial organs and magistracy — are constituted.

Aristotle's work contains many profound generalisations which can be applied to political life in all times and places. For instance, 'Man is a political man' and 'State came into being for the a sake of life, it continues for the sake of good life', were the themes underlying the thought of Plato, but Aristotle gave them their classical expression. To him, the purpose of the State was not to extend its dominion or enrich its people, but to widen knowledge, promote virtue and secure justice to all.

Besides emphasising on constitutionalism-making law the sovereign and governments the servants of law which gave inspiration to St. Thomas, Richard Hooker, Lock, Burke etc. Aristotle also realised that the ultimate problem of politics is the reconciliation of individual liberty and State authority. According to him, true liberty was not license but to live by the rule of the constitution or to obey, the rightly constituted law. But at the same time he laid stress on the value of public opinion. To him, the masses are better judges of the work of officials than the experts and, therefore, they should be given the right of final judgement. In other words, he locates the supreme power of sovereignty in the aggregate virtue and ability of the mass of the people is greater than the virtue and a ability of a part of the mass. This leads Aristotle to favour a vague sort of democracy. He would give ultimate sovereign power to the mass of citizens though the actual reigns of government would be in the hands of the best citizens only. To him, permanent exclusion of the multitude from all office is dangerous because it produces widespread discontent.

Aristotle differs from the current definition of democracy as the form of government in which the masses are supreme. According to him democracy is that form of government in which the poor, who constitute the majority, are supreme. It may also be defined as the polity based on the principles of civic equality and freedom. In order that the citizens be equal they must all have an equal right to share in the work of government. All the citizens are rulers as well as the ruled in turn. Elections to various offices are based on universal suffrage and are conducted by lot or rotation. Elections should have no property qualification or only nominal one. The tenure of offices should be short in order that all may be able to share them.

Aristotle has also guided the modern political science in analysing the governmental power into three organs — Executive, Legislative and Judicial, although his three elements of government — deliberative, magistracy and judicial organ — cannot be completely identified with them. Still Montesquieu drew a lot of inspiration from Aristotle in his theory of separation of powers. His remarkable political insight is also shown by his realisation of the inter-relation between politics and economics. He clearly explains the conflict between haves and have-nots. His classifications of governments and the distinctions between the various types of oligarchy and democracy ultimately hinge on economic issues. He goes on to show that stability and prosperity are secured easily in a State where there are no extremes of wealth and poverty and a strong middle class exists.

Aristotle's forms of government are sound and applicable even today to some extent. He was fully aware of the importance of economic element in producing conflicts. Perverted ideas of justice and inequality also cause revolutions. He gives a number of causes of revolution and also suggests remedies as to how the revolutions may be prevented. In this respect he influenced 'The Prince' of Machiavelli a lot.

The Politics of Aristotle exerted a profound influence on the thought of the Middle Ages and that of Christendom. He was known to have been called by Dante as the 'master of them that know'. In the words of Dunning, "The capital significance of Aristotle, in the history of political theories, lies in the fact that he gave to politics the character of independent science". It was accomplished by him by the disentanglement of political from ethical conceptions, whereas the two were completely blended in Plato's thought.

His doctrine of the golden mean is a precursor of the modern notion of political checks and balance. His good common sense and golden means led him to refute Platonic communism. His political philosophy is certainly more individualistic than that of Plato and as such he may be said to be the father of modern Individualism as well as the modern theory of popular sovereignty. According to Karl Frederick, Aristotle is the founder of Logic, of Political Science and of system of scholastics. Generally he has been of service to conservative and aristocratic critics of egalitarian democracy, to the historical and later to the sociological school. While Plato soared in the heights and later at the ideal, Aristotle's objective was not the ideally best but the best attainable. By his keen and practical political insight and systematic treatment of the subject Aristotle laid the foundations of real political science.

5

Aristotle's Criticism of Plato

Aristotle in Book II of the Politics, devotes himself to a critical study of the Ideal States projected by some writers like Phaleas of Chalcedon, Hippodamus of Miletus and Plato. But he mainly concentrates on Plato. This implies that the two philosophers are poles apart in their philosophies. His severest criticism of Plato is levelled against the following :

(1) Plato's conception of the unity of the State,

(2) Plato's Communism of Property and wives and

(3) Plato's neglect of lower classes in his ideal and sub-ideal states.

Almost the whole of Book II of the Politics is devoted to his criticism of Plato's Republic and the Laws according to Dunning.

(1) Plato's Conception of the Unity of State

Aristotle argues that the unity of States as emphasised by Plato would destroy that differentiation of function which the law of nature. He says that such a unified State would destroy the self-sufficiency of the State which is itself *raison d' etre.* He adds that since "the nature of a State is to be plurality, and leading to greater unity from being a State, it becomes a family, and from being a family, an individual." Attainment of greatest unity would be the destruction of the State. Similars do not constitute a State which is made up of different kinds of men. "A unity based on the removal of all diversities in individual is fatal to the state just as identity in musical tones is fatal to musical harmony."

According to Aristotle, unity lies in diversity. Real unity can be achieved in the State by proper organisation or relations among diverse individuals, who are complementary and supplementary to each other, because diversity of functions and organisation leads to exchange of services. This results in self-sufficiency and independence of the State. To Aristotle, Plato's system of State would, instead of creating a united and harmonious State, perpetuate disunity and discord because of two diverse and antagonistic elements of educated Guardians and uncultivated masses.

Aristotle is not fair in this criticism of Plato. Plato never sought to reduce the State to the unity of an individual. He clearly recognises the diversity of functions and interests in the State and accordingly provides three clearly distinguished classes. Platonic state is as much as organisation of diverse elements and in diverse relation to each other as the Aristotelian State. Uniformity of Platonic State, which is criticised by Aristotle, applies only to upper two classes and not to the majority of the population in the State, which belongs to the third class and is divided into sections with their diverse functions and interests.

(2) Plato's Communism of Property and Wives

Next criticism of Aristotle against Plato is regarding his communism of property and wives. Plato had suggested that his communism of property and wives was the means of creating unity and harmony in the State. Aristotle also considers unity of state as desirable, but he differs from Plato in its form and method of its achievement. He wants to create unity in the State by educating the people in the spirit of the constitution and not by the abolition of the time-honoured institution or private property and family. He believes in moderation, individual liberty and private property which are essential for the development of individuality and for the greatest good of the people.

According to Aristotle, common ownership of property tends to common neglect. What is everybody's interest is nobody's interest. People pay most attention to their own private property and less to that in which they have but a part interest. In a system of common property those who work hard and got little will have a grievance against those who work little and get much. There will be no incentive to work. Private property spurs men to greater activity and efficiency. No doubt, disputes arise in regard to private property but these are not due to its being private but to the wickedness of man. The defects of communism of property on the hand, spring from its nature and not from human wickedness. As in the case of people who travel together and have a common purse, they invariably come to quarrels, so by community of property such quarrels are most likely.

To Aristotle, the sense of property is a source of great pleasure as it is a form of self-love. Private property can be used for the benefit of friends etc. which gives happiness and opportunity for the exercise of the virtue of charity and benevolence. If men are deprived of property, they will have no attachment with the people and hence will lose all interest.

Property is essential so that man should perform his duties well. He considers that personal attachment alone will make men develop a sociable character. Aristotle advocates that property should be owned privately but must be shared in common and thereby secures the advantages of individualism and communism. Communism of property will upset the natural inequality of capacity and industry of individuals. Besides, human selfishness cannot be eradicated in this way, because it is embedded in the nature of men. It can be minimised only by properly educating the people to common use of their possessions. Denial of certain minimum of private property will thwart the fullest development of individuality and will result in the impoverishment of the whole state thereby. Private ownership brings economic and moral advantage and common use following from private spirit produces that unanimity which is desired the most. He is against the accumulation of wealth beyond the need of good life. He seeks to improve the institution of private property by proper custom and registration.

To Aristotle, Plato's Communism of wives is un-natural and foolish. Marriage is a holy institution. Private family is the basis of the state. Plato thinks that unity of State is best achieved when all the citizens lay 'mine' and 'thine', for the same things, *i.e.,* when all of them regard all the children as their own and no one has a separate home of his own. Thus, a man will feel an equally high affection for all the children in the State. But Aristotle objects that this communism will not result in greater love for all common children but no love for any, because the sense of personal possession and exclusive relationship is the only basis of affection. To him, the intensity of affection is inversely proportional to its extension. By extension it is reduced to watery friendship. The children will be neglected as everybody's business in nobody's business. He says that it is far better to be cousin than a Platonic son. In Platonic scheme each man will have a thousand sons and every child a thousand fathers. Public *creche* cannot substitute the home and the mother.

Community of wives signifies that every man's wife will be the wife of every other man. This will in practice breed discord and disharmony and give rise to jealousy. Moreover, all the guardians cannot be in actual possession of one wife. Again, under communism, unholy acts are likely to be committed against fathers or mothers, sisters or brothers because the relationship is unknown. At the same time, even in case of community of wives and children, it is impossible to prevent persons suspecting their own brothers, children, fathers and mothers. They are sure to derive proofs of mutual relationship from the likeness which the children bear to their parents.

While dealing with Aristotle's criticism of wives, we must bear in mind that Plato's system did not nationalise or socialise women in the Guardian classes but provided for temporary marriages between property selected pairs.

(3) Plato's Neglect of Lower Classes in his Ideal and Sub-Ideal States

Aristotle also criticises Plato for the neglect of non-Guardian classes, which form the over-whelming majority of the population of the State. He does not provide for any system of education for them, suiting their needs and requirements. In Plato's state, Guardian and non-Guardian classes will be hostile to each other. He has not stated their relation to each other. But we must bear in mind that though Aristotle criticises Plato's neglect of the lower classes whose existence he holds to be necessary for the State, he himself does not grant those classes right of citizenship in his Ideal State.

Aristotle's Criticism of the Laws of Plato

The Laws of Plato has been criticised by Aristotle on many grounds.

(1) Aristotle objects to the increase of warriors from 1000 to 5000 in Plato's sub-Ideal State as it will make the state too large. It will also tend to make it militaristic and imperialistic.

(2) He also points to the neglect of foreign relations in that state.

(3) Plato has not defined the amount of property. He should limit population which he does not do.

(4) Plato neglects to define the relation of the rulers to the ruled.

(5) Plato's council gives predominance to the rich classes.

(6) If other property may be increased more than four fold, why not land?

(7) Plato's system of double election will transfer the power of election into the hands of a clique.

(8) Plato allows two homesteads, one in the city and another in the border. But this will be very convenient.

(9) Plato in his sub-Ideal State does not mix tyranny with democracy which are obviously the worst of constitutions but mixed democracy and oligarchy.

(10) Aristotle says that Plato was not sincere about his sub-Ideal State as he reverts back to his early pet, the Ideal State of the Republic in the last Book of the Laws. Plato grudgingly accepts law to be supreme in his second best States *i.e.,* it was accepted as a concession to human family, but Aristotle has a firm conviction that law is the product of human progress.

Assessment. A large portion of Aristotle's criticism is inaccurate. His criticism of Plato's Ideal State is unfair, because Plato never wanted it to be actually put into practice, but to serve as an ideal to be followed. He regards it more as a measuring rod for State to judge their nature. Secondly, Plato has not destroyed differentiation of function because of his clear emphasis on the three classes in his Ideal State. Besides, his communism is also meant only for guardians. Moreover, many of Aristotle's ideas show that he is inconsistent in his philosophy, *i.e.,* what he criticises, he adopts latter, for instance, he says at places that a great majority of men are not natural dunces and sluggards; a State should lay down the best reasons for conception (children should be conceived in winter and that too when the wind is blowing in the North); infanticide may be replaced by abortion; teaching to the citizens that obedience to the State is the first obligation; offices should be reserved for the best equipped and so on. Salime says that his criticism of the Laws is inaccurate and "in his construction of the Ideal State, almost every subject discussed is suggested by the Laws and there are many parallelism (even verbal) in small points." So Jowett aptly points out that "The comments of Aristotle on Plato's Republic and Laws are full of inaccuracies and inconsistencies".

6

Aristotle's Theory of the State

Like Plato, Aristotle rejects the conventional theory of the origin of the state held by Sophists as an instrument, a mechanism, a piece of machinery to be used for purposes and ends higher than itself. He also rejects the theory of divine origin, the theory of force and the theory of social contract. Surprisingly enough, contractualists like Hobbes, Locke and Rousseau, totally forgot Aristotle's natural origin of State started controversy about its origin.

Origin of the State

According to Aristotle the state is to be found in the evolution of human nature. He believes that man is by nature a political animal. The State, according to him, is a natural institution. It is founded on the innate desire of an individual to satisfy his economic needs, and his social and racial instincts. For the realisation of the desire the male and the female on the one hand, and the master and the slave on the other, live together and form a family in a household, which has social and moral use. So long as the needs and desires are simple, it remains a separate unit. When the urge to seek a fuller life seizes the different households, they get pulled together into a village and then into a political state, which is big enough to be self-sufficient. The state is, therefore, a culmination of widening circle of human associations based on human wants. The state is not merely an economic association but also a moral community. It makes good life possible. Aristotle rightly said, "Man is a political animal, destined by nature for state life.....The State exists for the sake of good life, and not for the sake of life alone." As a matter of fact the state is a man's natural destination. The state is the highest form of association in terms of social value and purpose. It ensures self-sufficiency and promotes a good life. For Aristotle, the city-state was the highest unit of political organisation. He could not see beyond that.

Nature of the State

To Aristotle, the state is a political 'Koimonia'. The word 'Koimonia' has been translated as association, fellowship, partnership, reciprocity, community or communism. The State, according to him, is both a natural and a necessary institution. It is natural because its origin is in the very nature of man. Man by nature is a social animal. His natural gregariousness impels him to live in society. He looks towards the society for support because he cannot satisfy all his wants single handed. Thus, the state is natural for man and it is inherent in human nature. The satisfaction of an immanent impulse in human nature drives men towards moral perfection and finds it in the state after going through various forms of society.

The State is the end of other associations and the nature of a thing is its end. It is only in the state that all other associations and individuals can find true and final perfection. A rational being outside the state is neither perfect nor independent. It is only in the state alone that one finds perfection of life. It is only the state that can provide social peace and order, diversity of interests and a rich variety of life and province environment for leading a perfect life.

The state is natural also because it is man's destiny, his destination. It is natural also because outside of it a man is not self-sufficient. The individual is to the state as a part is to the whole. The state is necessary for man because it serves not only a man's animal nature but also his rational one. The state is also the product of reason as it is the culmination of the evolution of man's nature. Animals unite by sensation but men unite by reason, having the power of speech. It is the characteristic of man that he can distinguish between good and evil, just and unjust. In this sense the state is the product of reason.

The End of the State

As regards the end of the state, Aristotle believed that it was the attainment of the supreme good. The end was positive. According to him the state does not exist merely for the sake of providing security against external or internal danger, not only for the sake of exchange of services and mutual intercourse. The state is there to ensure a perfect and self-sufficing life.

Its end is good life. One of the functions of the state is the education of its citizen in virtue. The state must provide the means and the media to the individual for the attainment of intellectual, moral and physical excellence. So, the state was "a spiritual association in a moral life." The good life which the state must help the individual to attain requires three types of good; external such as wealth, slaves, leisure etc., physical, such as the attainment of health; and spiritual, such as attainment of virtue and morality. Poverty destroys good impulses; ill-health retards virtuous action. Leisure based on possession of property, was necessary for moral action and civic duty.

Organic Character of the State

Aristotle regards the state as an organism. As an organism consists of different parts, in the same way, the 'state is the whole' composed of a number of organs representing elements of diverse structure, character and functions which are parts of and dependent on the whole. As the human organism has its integral parts like hands and feet etc., and contributing parts like blood and bones, the state too has integral parts like the military, judicial, sacerdotal and deliberative classes representing the body of citizens and contributory organs like cultivators, artisans, labourers and traders who are non-citizens. The state like individual, is a moral agent. A group of individuals forming, the state has the same happiness and virtues and aims as the individual. Then Aristotle identifies the state with its constitution and, therefore, to change the constitution is to change the State itself. Aristotle identified the state with its constitution because he believed that it was 'form', which was definite and knowable and not "matter" which was in a state of constant flux, that constituted the identity of a thing.

Difference between State and Government

Aristotle was the first to bring out the distinction between the state as an assemblage of the body of citizens, and the government which consists of those citizens alone who hold the supreme political power and administer the state. The government is a tangible means of attaining the ends and performing the moral and political functions of the state. While the government would change with the overthrow of those who occupy the highest political offices, the state changed only when its constitution was changed. Aristotle did not believe the sovereignty of the state. Sovereignty belonged to the *de facto* government of the state.

Forms of Government

According to Aristotle the government in a state could be constituted on the basis of three features *viz.*, (1) birth, (2) wealth and (3) number.

The first case has this defect *i.e.,* one monarch may be wise, good and efficient ruler, his successor may prove to be moral or intellectual degenerate.

Secondly, a government based on wealth may not be good or efficient because wealth is no criterion of moral, intellectual or political worth.

The third basis is one of number. To him the aggregate virtue and ability of the mass of the people is greater than the virtue and ability of a part of that mass. They have sense enough to choose the right type of rulers for themselves and should be able to bring to book their rulers, if the latter misbehaved. So he was in favour of a vogue sort of democracy as the best practical form of government.

Aristotle's classification of state is both quantitative and qualitative. In the first case, the form of the state is determined by the number of persons who enjoy political power in the state — one, few or many. It is qualitative when the form of the state is determined by the end of the state and the spirit of the government.

The second basis makes a distinction between the pure and perverted form of states and governments. If the state follows the end as the common good of the whole community, it is said to be normal, and if it does not follow this end it is said to be perverted. On these two bases, the state can be of six kinds : normal as well as perverted; three pure forms : *monarchy* — with promotion of supreme virtue as its guiding principle; *aristocracy* — representing a mixture of virtue and wealth; *polity* — representing partial and medium virtues, power resting mainly with middle class people. Three perverted or corrupt forms : *tyranny* — based on deceit and selfishness. *Oligarchy* — representing greed of wealth; *democracy* — representing the principle of equality, liberty and majority rule with power in the hands of the many poor.

Aristotle is not in favour of monarchy as it is beset with difficulties of perpetuation. Excellence of character and intellect cannot be passed on to successors. The Rule of Law is the rule of reason and of God and so is better than the will of the monarch, unlimited monarchy is against the principle of human equality.

Aristocracy is also difficult of realisation.

Polity, the rule of the many for the good of all can also got perverted into democracy.

Organisation of Government

Aristotle believes that three institutions must obtain in a state to perform the three main functions : deliberative, executive and judicial. For the first, there must be a popular assembly consisting of all citizens, for the second there must be a system of magistracy and a judicial system for performing the judicial function. He does not want his to be thrown open to all citizens. He is for a form of government in which a property qualification for holding office is laid down. It will bring more efficiency, stability and harmony — Thus, Aristotle stands for the rule of the middle classes and follows the rule of the golden mean.

Criticism

The theory of the state as given by Aristotle is not free from shortcomings. Firstly, his organic conception makes it a mighty leviathan which has no regard and respect for individuals.

Secondly, it is neither a satisfying explanation of the state nor a trust-worthy guide to state activity.

Finally, some of his views on state are built upon wrong assumptions.

On the whole, his theory has been accepted by almost all modern thinkers, though with some modifications. The modern world is increasingly realising the truth of the Aristotelian end of the state. His classification of Governments, though not very comprehensive, is still followed by every political philosopher. His state is teleological as it exists for the sake of life and for a purpose which is good life.

7

The Politics of Aristotle

If in his *Ethics,* Aristotle discusses the nature of individual happiness, in the *Politics* he treats of the state as one of the chief aims through which an individual attains his happiness. According to Jowett "the object of the *Politics* is both practical and speculative; to explain the nature of the ideal city in which the end of happiness may be completely realised to suggest some methods of making existent states more useful to the individual citizen than they were in Aristotle's time, or had been in the past".

The *Politics* has always served as a pillar of light for all those who came after Aristotle and it has been a great source of inspiration to all the political scientists of the world. Its subject matter is not only theoretical, it is of great practical utility. It may be called a treatise on the art of government.

According to Foster, "The *Politics* of Aristotle is a work of such practical reason. It is a hand-book for the statesman containing the wisdom distilled, as it were, from the collective political experience of the Greek-States."

The object of the whole study was to find out such constitutional laws and principles on the basis of which such a constitution to be drafted which could be stable and which could stand the best of time.

Prof. Bowle holds that *Politics* of Aristotle "is the most influential and most profound. It is a book which must be mastered before all others." It is in fact the richest store of political knowledge.

The *Politics* of Aristotle cannot be regarded as a finished work. It is a heap of arrangements and theories, sometimes repeated or left unfinished rather than an artistically done piece of literature. None of the manuscripts of the works of the Master available to us, is older than the 12th or 13th century A.D. and there are many variations or corruptions of these works. These works appear to be either notes taken down by his pupils or rough notes prepared by Aristotle himself. The political writings of Aristotle are confined to his Nicomachean Ethics, but chiefly to his *Politics.* Both the Ethics and Politics are guide to constitution-makers, for securing happiness, *i.e.,* life of complete virtue. Politics is, therefore, more a book on the art of Government than a systematic exposition of political philosophy.

The only city-states whose constitution Aristotle makes use of his Politics, are Athens, Sparta, Crete and Carthage.

The only writers whcm Aristotle makes reference to by way of acknowledgement are Plato, Hippodamus and Phalleas.

In short, the sketch of the ideal state remains unfinished.

It is not known what was the original arrangement of the Book, *The Politics*. According to Wilamowitz the book consists of three divisions. But according to the traditional arrangement the *Politics* consisting of eight Books, is roughly divisible into three — one scholar by name W.D. Ross makes five — related parts but different in points or view and the methods of treatment. These three divisions, according to Earnest Barker and others are :

(1) A 'common foundation' for the subject (Books I, II and III giving rise to two construction independent of each other),

(2) "Explanation of the nature of constitutions, the distinctions between and the changes within them" (Books IV, V and VI).

(3) "The principles underlying the best state" (Books VII and VIII).

The Book I, the general introduction, opens with an enquiry into the nature of the state. He also examines the structure of the household, the question of property and the nature and position of a slave, whom he defines as one "by nature not his own, but another's a human being but also a possession." Being the child of his times, he takes slavery for granted.

The Book II deals with Plato's Ideal State and States projected by less eminent philosophers and with the constitution of Sparta, Crete and Carthage.

The Book III describes the main forms of constitutions normal as well as perverted, and deals fairly exhaustively with monarchy.

The Book IV reviews forms of government other than monarchy and deals not only with main types but also with sub-special and varieties.

The Book V deals with the causes of revolutions and their preventions. Inferiors revolt in order that they may be equal, and equals that they may be superior. Aristotle is fully aware of the importance of economic element in producing conflict. But the general causes of revolution might be found in the perverted ideas of justice.

The Book VI describes the organisation of democracies and oligarchies. The best kind of democracy is agricultural, for few farmers want the nuisance of office. Mob democracy in the worst and finds many supporters since 'most persons would rather live in a disorderly than in a sober manner'. Demogogues maintain their power by bribing the electorate. Then he discusses the right distribution of offices and the need to audit public accounts.

The Book VII, which should have been put after Book III is a return to the construction of the best State and general principles. This book "is one of the wisest achievements of the Greek mind." "True happiness is," says Aristotle, 'more often found with those who are most highly cultivated in mind and character'. He insists on the small size of the state, for experience shows to him that very large states cannot be very well governed. He advocates common meals in the weil ordered city. True happiness depends on right type of education, which should foster reason and control appetite. Marriage should take place at the age of 18 for women and 37 for men. He advocates birth control by abortion to avoid over population. "Let there be a law that no deformed child shall live".

The Short Book VIII, after a further enquiry into the principles of education, is mainly concerned with the function of music.

According to Warner Jaeger, a reputed scholar of Aristotle, the Politics was written in two stages. The first stage covers the works dealing with the Ideal State and with previous theories of it. This includes Book-II, representing a historical study of earlier theories of State and criticism of Plato, Book III, being a study of the nature of the state and citizenship, and Books VII and VIII dealing with the construction of the best, *i.e.,* Ideal State. The second stage relates to the work dealing with a study of actual states, mainly democracies and oligarchies, causes of their decay and finding means of their stability which is covered by Books IV, V and VI.

Jaeger holds that Books IV, V and VI were inserted in the middle of the original drafts to give it the shape of general treatise on political science. Book I was written last by way of introduction. The entire work took about 15 years. In the first stage is evident the influence of Plato's idealism while the second stage shows emancipation from this influence. In the first stage, Aristotle is constructing the Ideal State after the model of the Laws. In the second stage he conceives of politics in a mere general sense.

Assessment

The Book covers a wide range of subjects; political science, education, ethics, jurispondence, psychology and economics. It is meant for both politicians as well as moral, ethical thinkers. The ideas in the book are universally acceptable. Aristotle's statement that 'the state comes into existence for the sake of life, but it continues to exist for the sake of good life' explains the theory of political obligation which, today, has been accepted as the moral basis of all democratic governments. The philosophers of the scientific, pragmatic, utilitarian and historical schools of thought have borrowed much from the teachings of Aristotle as contained in the *Politics*. "His *Politics* came to be for European philosophy what the Bible was for theology. It influenced Christian thought enormously. St. Thomas Acquinas, Marsiglio of Padua, Machiavelli of the middle ages and Bodin, Montesquieu and Harrington of the modern age, all bear the impress of Aristotelian thought. There is no doubt that Ethics and Politics of Aristotle are a guide to constitution makers and will remain so in order to enable them to provide the best possible politics for securing happiness — a life of complete virtue.

8

Aristotle's Theory of Justice

Aristotle like his master Plato, believed that 'justice' is the very essence of the state and that no policy can endure for a long time unless it is founded on a right scheme of justice. However, he removes the shortcomings and imperfections of the Platonic theory of justice and gives out a new brand. Aristotle regards justice as a complete virtue. A completely just man is a completely virtuous man. Justice for Aristotle is the name of that great moral virtue and excellence of character which is so very necessary for dealing with social and public relations. This is complete justice. A just and law-abiding citizen is one and the same. And since being law-abiding is a complete virtue, justice is also a complete virtue.

Distributive justice is that principle of distribution by which goods, services, honour and offices are distributed among the citizens of the state. Since every citizen of the state makes a contribution to thc realization of the common life, it is necessary that he must get back the contribution in proportion to the amount and kind of contribution made by him to the life of the state. Different men make different contributions and hence their claims are different. But every state fixes its own standard for measuring the worth and due of a man. The due of a man depends upon his contribution to the life of the community for making it happy and self-sufficient. How to measure the contribution is a ticklish problem. Aristotle, however, feels that the most virtuous should have the most power. His distributive justice is another name for proportionate equality. It recognizes and preserves the distinction between the worthy and the non-worthy. It counters equality of the unequal and ensures that a man's rights, duties and rewards should correspond to his merit and social contribution.

Justice in the state is relative and not absolute. Corrective justice aims to see that the proportionate equality so established by distributive justice is not disturbed. Corrective justice prevents an individual from making encroachment upon the right of his fellows. Thus, particular justice guarantees the province of each individual against every other, and secures to each individual his proper position as a part of the whole.

Plato and Aristotle, however, differ in their conceptions. Aristotle's justice lays emphasis on a system of rights, while Platonic justice gives importance to duties. Aristotle's justice is based on the principle that 'everyone should have his own', whereas Platonic justice is based on the principle that 'everyone should do his own'.

Then Aristotle's justice is legal in character as the legal side is represented by corrective justice. Platonic justice, on the other hand, is essentially moral and philosophical and is based on idealism far removed from reality.

Thirdly, Aristotle's justice established equality between different members of the state, whereas Platonic justice establishes a hierarchy of classes, where every citizen is bound to his duties in his class.

Lastly, Aristotle's justice is based on a classification of complete and particular justice, whereas Plato makes no such classification. The aim of both, however, is the same : to find out the principle of capacity through which unity, harmony and happiness can be established in the state.

Aristotle's justice and modern conception of justice are more or less the same, though both differ on certain aspects. Both lay emphasis on rights and duties but modern conception gives classification of rights, social, political, economic, legal and fundamental, whereas Aristotle makes no such classification. Again, both conceptions are founded on equality but the modern concept of equality, social, political and legal was beyond the comprehension of Aristotle. Both conceptions issue forth in juridical organization. The aim of both is attainment of complete happiness. Thus, both the conceptions are legal as well as ethical.

9

Aristotle's Theory of Education

Virtue and goodness in a State is not a matter of chance but the result of knowledge and purpose. Animals are creators of habit, but man alone has reason. Education should foster reason that it may control appetite. The perfection of the community depends upon the perfection of its constituent members, and the perfection of the latter can be achieved only through the cultivation of moral and intellectual excellence. Hence, a system of uniform compulsory public education, without any regard for birth or occupation, is the first essential of the best State and the administration of such a system is the most important function of government. Aristotle's project of educational legislation is of the same general character as that of Plato. It aims at mental culture rather than practical utility; lays due stress upon the physical side of the training and attaches to music a moral significance and a character making influence, education is same to all. The educational system is calculated to make good citizens soldiers and administrators.

Although education actually starts from the age of seven, but Aristotle, like Plato, starts with the unborn baby. As stated above, he gives his rigid regulations for time and conditions of marriage and procreation and care of infants. From birth till the end of the 7th year, children are to be properly fed and given muscular exercises. They should be trained to withstand the rigours of climate. They should be given plenty of milk, which is the best food for human beings. Upto the age of 5, children should only play but with the games which are miniature representations of the later life. They should be kept away from bad company and indecency of speech and must not go to the theatre until they are of an age 'to sit at the public table and drink — strong wine'. They must be allowed exercise and amusement, so long as it is not vulgar. According to Aristotle, Plato is wrong 'in attempting to check the loud crying and screaming of children. For those contribute towards their growth and in a manner exercise their bodies. In the next period, they should be made to learn by doing things instead of reading about them.

After early childhood, stress should be placed on gymnastics for beauty, grace and symmetry of body. Then music should be taught, which is not only amusement but a moral discipline and a rational form of enjoyment. Children should hear those modes that promote ethical behaviour, Music reinforces the physical development made by gymnastics and produces a sound mind in a sound body. In early manhood the citizens should be educated for the service of the State, being taught to obey when young and rule when old. On first becoming citizens they should study philosophy in a practical way. With growth of age they should be assigned posts of less activity and more thought, till they devote themselves exclusively to speculative philosophy, the highest of human developments. The very old, who approach nearest to the gods, become priests and live in communion with them.

According to Aristotle, education should begin with the body first, then with appetite and lastly with reason. His educational system runs in cycles of seven years. In the first 7 years of infancy education is at home. In next two periods of 7 years each, the state takes charge of the pupil. From seven to puberty the emphasis is on a proper development of the body, while from puberty to the age of 21 cultivation of mind receives special attention. Like Plato, Aristotle age limits that education should be controlled by State, which will bring uniformity in it and which will instruct the citizens in the spirit of its constitution. His system of education is confined to the citizens only and thereby Aristotle is guilty for creating a charm between the citizens and non citizens bodies in the State. It is in nut-shell Aristotle's system of education which he proposes to introduce in the best State in order to make a citizen socially, morally and politically high.

To sum up, Aristotle's best State is 'neither too rich nor too poor', secure from attach and devoid of the desire for great or wide expansion of trade or territory, "homogeneous, virtuous and cultured, a defensible unambitious community, self-sufficient but not aggressive great but not large; a tight little independent city over which the supreme power will rest in a true aristocracy." In this best practicable State he firmly reputes the assertion that laws and moral are matters of convention. Here once again he is one with Plato in considering laws to be a thing higher than the common custom and usage.

Aristotle's best State, as conceived above, seems to be a typical Greek State of Aristotle's days. In spite of his vast knowledge and long stay in the capital of the Macedonian empire he could not suggest a bigger state, nor could be put forward the idea of a federation or a confederation. Their pity is that Greek politics, despite the fact that they had the best of the brains world has ever produced, could not last long, and soon fell the prey to other States, this is on the charges that are generally levied against Aristotle. His State is defective in one other way also. He allowed the institution of slavery to exist. For us today, it is a great slur on the name of democracy but he had reasons to support and justify its existence, with the end of Book VIII, not only in the subject of education left unfinished but Aristotle makes no mention of the actual governmental machinery of his ideal States. It maybe due to a part of the Politics having been lost to us.

Despite all these defects, the world is indebted to Aristotle for the idea of democracy that he initiated. Not only this, Aristotle has also been regarded as the founder of the three departments of the State-Executive, Legislative and Judiciary. To conclude, Aristotle's best State is defective in certain respects no doubt but at the same time, it forms a precedent upon which rests to great extent, the modern system of government.

10

Aristotle's Theory of Family and Property

Family is the smallest unit of the State. It is the basis for the origin of the State. Aristotle tries to examine its nature and constituents. While determining the nature of property and household the following facts must be taken into account :

(1) Plato is of the opinion that a small State and a great household are essentially the same and 'the government of both is but one science'. But Aristotle disagrees with this view.

(2) It was Aristotle who, first of all, worked out the fundamental principle that the character and distribution of wealth is a determining factor in fixing the form of government.

Aristotle holds that every citizen requires private property and the discipline of family life. He regards them as institutions belonging to all by the order of nature.

Definition of Property

Property according to Aristotle "in the sense of a bare livelihood, seems to be given by nature herself to all, both when they are grown-up."

Aristotle is of the opinion that property is of two kinds. They are : (i) Inanimate and (ii) Animate.

According to Aristotle property may be either private or local, private property must be protected by the State otherwise somebody else will take possession of it.

Private property is necessary for the existence and proper functioning of the household. Maxey supports it in these words, "as nature's own way of assuring man the wherewithal to live. The things which are necessary for life such as food, clothing and shelter constitute property. The instinct of acquiring property in man is natural. But the amount of property required by the family is limited by its needs, to have in excess is bad as to have less than what is required."

According to Foster, "A hammer must be heavy in order to serve its purpose; but the object of the hammer — maker will not be to make it as heavy as possible. The same function of the hammer which demands weight also, sets a limit to the weight required; and the good hammer maker will observe this limit. The essence of Aristotle's saying is that all true wealth must be limited."

His Justification of Private Property

Aristotle advocates the following grounds for the justification of private property :

(i) For social economy private property is very essential. Aristotle says, "when everyone has a distinct interest, men will make more progress because every one will be attending to his own business."

Ebenstein is of the view that Aristotle links the idea of self-interest with that of social progress. Where self-interest is involved, the individual concerned will do his best and his best efforts will in turn benefit the society.

(ii) The instinct of acquiring property is the nature's gift to man.

(iii) The need and necessity of property is emphasised here. It is necessary for the proper functioning of the household. According to Maxey, "it is nature's own way of assuring man the wherewithal to live."

(iv) Private property makes the man know the art of managing it and the experience thus gained will also be useful in the management of State affairs.

(v) The ownerships of private property creates a sense of civic responsibility in the owner.

(vi) The instinct of private property is essential for leading good life as well as for the development of individual personality.

(vii) The ownership of property is a source of pleasure. Aristotle says, "Almost all men love money." Thus, on psychological ground also Aristotle defends private property.

According to Aristotle the following are the three modes of holding and using property :

(1) Private property in land but common use of the produce.

(2) Common property and private use.

(3) Common property and common use.

Aristotle has preferred the first mode. He says, "It is clearly better that property should be private but the use of it common."

Aristotle criticises Plato's communism of property by pointing out that in a system of common property those who work hard and get little will have a grievance against those who work little and get much. Common ownership of property is a great source of dispute as among fellow travellers. Men are more efficient when set to work at that which is their own. The sense of property is a source of great pleasure, being a form of self-love. The use of property to help one's friends is a further source of pleasure and affords an opportunity for the exercise of the virtue of charity and benevolence. The quarrels that arise over private property are due not to its being private but to the wickedness of human nature.

Plato's communism applies to the guardians only. Aristotle denounces Plato's communism of property — and advocates the system of common use based on private property. Things belonging to all belong to none, for exclusive possession is different from a fractional interest.

To Aristotle, to communise property is to try to get rid of human selfishness by ineffective social legislation. Selfishness cannot be easily eradicated because it is embedded in the nature of man. The best cure for this selfishness is education in the spirit of the constitution which will lead men to use their private wealth generously and induce them to freely allow the common use of what they own individually.

According to Aristotle every one needs a certain minimum of private property for self-realisation and self-expression. To deny this minimum, to which an individual may have free access, is to thwart the fullest development of individuality. The consequent loss is not only individual, it impoverishes the whole state.

His Views on Family

Plato's communism of wives does not appeal to Aristotle. He holds that Plato's theory as un-natural and fantastic. To Aristotle, family is a natural association of which man becomes a member from the time of his birth. It is as natural as the State. Marriage is a holy institution and family is the basis of the State. Household constitutes the historical origin of the State.

Aristotle also does not agree with Plato's view that a small State and a big household are essentially the same and the Government of both is also the same..

Certainly the State and the family are not the same. They differ greatly, Family satisfies the elementary needs of the man. It exists for satisfying the physical needs of man while the State satisfies the moral and intellectual needs. It is an association of associations and the highest of all.

11

Aristotle on Slavery

Aristotle's conception of a slave follows his theory of the state as a derivative of the household. The household economy necessitates the possession of instruments which are of various kinds — living and lifeless. The former are slaves and servants. According to Aristotle, a slave is a living possession and an instrument of action. A slave is not only a slave to his master, he wholly belongs to him, "for he who can be and, therefore, is another's and who participates in reason enough to comprehend but not to have reason, is a slave by nature." The slave differs from the master in not possessing reason, and from lower-animals in being able to comprehend it.

Aristotle's theory of slavery depends on two postulates :

(1) By nature men are unequal and divided with respect to their capacities for virtue.

(2) That is possible to determine who is virtuous and who is not virtuous.

Nature of Slavery

Delivering in the natural inequality of mankind, Aristotle held that slavery was natural and based on justice. He holds, "for that some should rule and others be ruled is a thing, not only necessary, but expedient; from the hour of their birth, some one marked out for subjection, others for rule." Aristotle contends that 'nature is universally ruled by the contrast of the superior and inferior : man is superior to animals, the male to the female, the soul to the body and reason to passion. In all these divisions, the superior rules over the inferior.' It is from actual causes that some being command and others obey, that each may obtain their mutual safety, for being who is endowed with a mind capable of reflection and fore-thought is by nature the superior and governor, whereas he whose excellence is merely corporal is formed to be a slave; hence, it follows that the different state of master and slave is equally advantageous to both. Just as mind governs the body with political and kindly power to mutual advantage, so must the master govern the slave.

His Justification of Slavery

Aristotle justifies the institution of slavery on the following grounds :

(1) Natural inequality of mankind — Aristotle is of the view that men are by nature inequal with respects to their capacities for virtue. Nature has not endowed men with similar quantities. Nature desires that men should be mentally and physically equal. There are persons who possess high sense of reason and who are fit to command, while there are others whose intellectual standard is low and who are fit to obey only. Nature with that the former type of people be masters and the latter slaves. Thus, we see, slavery in accordance with nature.

(2) Superiors rule over inferiors — Aristotle's views, in this respect is mentioned above very clearly.

(3) Slavery is just one more manifestation of the general rule of nature of the subordination of the inferior to the superior. In the words of Mulwain, "Slavery, in short, is only one more manifestation of the general rule of nature. But wherever several parts combine to form a whole, there invariably appears a subordination of some of these parts to others, a relation of rule and subject of some kind, as of man over man, is man over by the beasts, the soul over the body.....and if this subjection is natural, it is just."

(4) According to Aristotle, a master in order to lead a good life needs slaves.

(5) Slavery secures the best conditions for the slave, hence, it has been justified by Aristotle.

(6) Sophists like Antiphone and Alcidamus are of the opinion that slavery is an isolation of nature. They deem the institution of slavery unjust because it exists by convention and not by nature. They held that all men are equal. Contrary to this, Aristotle seeks to justify slavery but with certain conditions. These conditions are :

(i) A distinction should be made between a slave by nature and a slave by law.

(ii) Aristotle does not approve of slavery by law.

(iii) Aristotle says that the master while dealing with the slave must not misuse his authority. With this slave, he should behave like a friend.

(iv) The slaves should be given the hope and also opportunity of emancipation.

(v) A Greek should not enslave a Greek except casually. This was because of the widespread feeling among Greeks that they ought to hold in slavery only persons of other races. The inherent intellectual superiority of the Hellenes over the barbarians was one of the primary and universal exioms of Greek thought which Aristotle was in agreement with.

(vi) Aristotle admits that the distinction between the natural free man and the natural slave is not always as clear as might be wished. Nor is the child of a natural slave always a natural slave.

(vii) The prisoners of war should be enslaved only if they are intellectually inferior to their victors. Rightful masters should not be reduced to slavery by accident as a result of war. Slavery by law was not always justifiable because in a state which was not ideal, law may be bad and may unjustly enslave people.

Aristotle's Position

During the period of Aristotle, there were some Greeks who maintained that slave hunting was a lawful employment, necessitated by considerations of national economy. There were, on the other hand, anti-slaveryites particularly the Sophists, who assorted that freedom was the birth right of all individuals. Aristotle shrank from either of these two extremes. He would neither allow slave-hunting nor moralise over the abolition of the institution of slavery.

During this period complete emancipation of slaves was not warranted by the conditions and social economy of the time. Aristotle proposes the emancipation of individual slaves as a reward for good conduct. Then again, Aristotle's suggestion to open a career to slaves is in advance of any modern practice. Aristotle would emancipate a slave who has developed his reason and capacity for self-direction.

To him, in an imperfect state all slaves are not rightful slaves. It is inconceivable that a barbarian should have a Greek slave. He further says that in his time the condition of Athenian slave was uncomfortable. He dressed like his master; he was treated as a member of the family in his owner's household, who, legally and socially, was not degraded and who was protected by the state, some of these Athenian slaves merely paid annual rent to their masters. They could by their emancipation and generally filled the lower posts in the civil service. It must also be borne in mind that while justifying natural slavery suitable rejects legal slavery. Slavery is natural because of its ethical value. The slave becomes a moral being supplemented with the moral faculty of his master. Besides, civilisation requires an order of things in which some do intellectual, some mere manual work.

Criticism

Aristotle has been bitterly criticised for his justification of slavery on the following grounds :

(1) Aristotle holds that human beings are dividable into two classes — superior and inferior. According to him superiors are those who are endowed with the capacity for virtue while inferiors are those lacking this

quality. But human beings cannot be divided into two such classes. It cannot be said that any person or a group of persons lacks the capacity for virtue entirely.

(2) There is contradiction in his views. On the one hand, he recommends a humane treatment of slaves by the master, while, on the other, he treats slaves as an animate instrument of action who cannot apply reason.

(3) Aristotle holds that all non-Greeeks are barbarious and consequently he is of the opinion that war prisoners, if they are not Greeks; may be justifiably made slaves. This view cannot be justified by any canon. It seems that Aristotle's views on slavery are evolved due to his radical prejudice.

(4) Aristotle has simply said that human beings are dividable into two classes but he has not fixeed any criterion for this purpose. In such a case, now it is to be determined whether a person belongs to the superior class or to thee inferior class.

(5) Division of society in two classes is bound to cause disturbance and disorder.

(6) Aristotle's emphasis on heredity also does not stand to reason. His opinion that some persons are by nature slaves is not convincing. We all know that environment plays an important role. Besides, it would be totally wrong to say that a slave has no reason. A slave also possesses some reason and if proper facilities and environment are obtaining, it can certainly be developed.

(7) Aristotle holds that some people are born to command and others to obey. If this view is deemed right, then a vast majority of the people today would be slave.

(8) Freedom and equality is the slogan of the present day and Aristotle's justification of the institution of slaveery is the very negation of this slogan.

(9) Aristotle says, "Nature ordains that the superiors should command and inferiors should obey." But in such a case there will not only be two classes in the society but countless, becausee every person in the same way or the other will be supeerior to some one and inferior to other.

12

Aristotle on Citizenship

The determination of the question of citizenship has been a very important problem since the dawn of political speculation. In ancient Greece citizenship entitled a man to the membership of the city-state which included a minimum share in political activity. The range of this political activity depended on the democracy prevailing in the city-state.

Aristotle discusses this problem in Book III of his politics, we come to its central and most fundamental question, *i.e.,* Aristotle's conception of Citizenship and of the State.

Book III opens with the question, What is a 'State'? To Aristotle, the state was, viewed objectively, an assemblage of citizens. But who is a citizen? Aristotle, in his attempt to define a citizen, proceeds negatively, by assembling that (1) A residence in a particular place does not make a citizen because resident aliens and slaves, if any, also live in the same state. (2) The right of suing and being sued also does not make a citizen, for this may be secured to resident aliens by treaty. Such persons are citizens only in a qualified sense as are those who are too old or too young to be citizens proper. (3) Those who are disenfranchised or exiled are not citizens. (4) Descent from a citizen is not what makes a citizen, for if this were a necessary qualification, what about the first citizen?

Aristotle's Definition of a Citizen

Aristotle analyses the conception of citizenship into its essential and non-essential attributes. An essential attribute is one which a citizen must and a citizen alone can possess. The essential attribute of citizenship is neither residence, descent nor legal privilege but civic function, not for a limited but an indefinite period.

The question 'who is a citizen' is answered by Aristotle with reference to a purely Hellenic fact. To him, a citizen is one who participates in the administration of justice and in legislation as a member of the deliberative assembly, either — or both these being the two essential functions of sovereignty. Aristotle's citizen, therefore, was one who partook of the duty of functioning as a juror or taking part in the deliberations of the state assemblies. Citizenship, thus, signifies the enjoyment of political rights and duties and the state was coincident with the group of persons exercising there rights and duties.

Aristotle realised that governments and states differed in kind and in constitution and pointed out that the definition of a citizen given above was applicable to democracies only. The definition of a citizen must differ according to the form of government. In oligarchies, for instance, holders of certain definite offices but not all citizens took part in legislation and served as jurors.

Aristotle's conception of citizenship is less democratic and more exalted than that of Plato. To plato, the citizen-body included the entire passive, uneducated, and non-political demos of the city-state, whereas Aristotle's citizen is an active agent capable of political speculation and actively participating in public life. He must have the capacity to rule and be ruled. Aristotle's citizen was the head of a household with enough of property and leisure to be able to devote himself to public affairs.

Women, children, slaves and aliens and men with commercial pursuits could not become citizens. Manual work deliberalized the soul and incapacitated it for enlightened and civic virtue. Property was necessary for citizenship, not only because it afforded leisure for speculation and public work but also because it created an interest and stake in the safety of the state. Aristotle discards the Platonic view that the capacity to rule is the exclusive monopoly of few individuals, *i.e.,* guardians, and yet he is more reactionary than Plato, for whereas the latter makes the producing classes an organic part of the state, the former makes them instruments and not members of the state.

Virtue of Citizenship

Connected with the question "who is a citizen" is a further question whether the virtues of the good citizen are identical with virtues of the good man. The virtues and excellence of all citizens are not the same since they have to perform different functions in the state though they have a common object, the safety and good government of the state. Since the forms of government differ and the virtues of citizen in a democracy are different from those in an oligarchy, the good citizen everywhere cannot have the perfect and absolute virtue of the good man. The good man, like a good ruler, is given to moral wisdom, *i.e.,* conscious moral self-guidance. Therefore, the virtues of good man are identical with the virtues of a good ruler, but may be different from those of a good citizen.

A good citizen may be a good man. In a perfect state, while every one is a good citizen, he may not be a good man, unless we assume that all the citizens in such a state are alike. But there can be cases where virtues of a good citizen and a good man are identical. For instance, a good and wise man. A good citizen may not only be the equal of but superior to the good man. Each polity has its moulding influence on civic virtue and citizenship. Good citizenship connoted different things in different politics. This is because each policy "embodied a scheme of life, and tended consciously or not to bring the lives of those living under it into harmony with its particular scheme."

Qualification for Citizenship

Aristotle holds that the prime qualification for citizenship is the capacity to rule and be ruled in turn. Are mechanics and labourers fit to be classed as citizens? No, because, insists Aristotle, a citizen must develop the two fold capacity to rule and be ruled and possess virtue. Those who must labour to live are too dependent on the command of others to develop the capacity of commanding others. Besides, freedom from cares and worries about the necessities of life is indispensable for the proper performance of the political duties of a juror and a legislator attached to citizenship. The working classes are necessary for the state but they cannot be granted citizenship because they have neither the ability nor the leisure of performing political duties properly. An essential qualification for citizenship, to Aristotle, was the holding of property which alone could ensure leisure necessary for participation in civic duties. It is obvious that in holding his view, Aristotle was reacting against and censuring practice in contemporary Athens of payment of citizens for performance of their public duties which vitiated public standards and brought in the evils of democracy.

According to Aristotle, a citizen must have leisure. Life is made up of work, recreation and leisure. To Aristotle, leisure in not relaxation but activity but not the activity of work. Work is an activity which is a means to a desirable end but which would not be undertaken for its own sake as, for instance, cultivation. But leisure is an activity worth undertaking for its own sake because through it a man exercises and perfects his human virtue. These activities of leisure include political speculation, performance of public services, etc.

The Essence of Citizenship

In answering the question as to what is the essence of citizenship or what is it to be a citizen, Aristotle relies partly on his own reasoning and partly on the then current meaning of the word. A citizen must be an active member of a city-state and not a mere resident and adherent nor a mere means to its existence. What are the minimum functions of a member of the state? These are to be a juryman and a member of the Assembly. These functions assigned by Aristotle to a citizen do not admit of universal application. There may be states in which the jury system does not obtain.

Again, it is not the membership of the sovereign assembly that should constitute the essence of true citizenship. This criterion will lose its force in a state with representative government. Aristotle, of course, agrees that true citizenship differs in different forms of government. The service to the service of a citizen is not service of a slave or a mechanic but the service of a free man in a constitutional state.

Criticism

(1) Aristotle's conception of a citizen is widely different from the modern conception of the word. This is mainly because Aristotle conceived of a citizen in a city state where there often was, and could be, direct democracy and where the social and political conditions differed form those that obtain in modern country-states. His conception, therefore, is not applicable to a modern state, particularly one with representative government.

(2) Aristotle assigns to his citizen the functions of a juror and a legislator. As noted above, there may be system of government where there is no jury system. Again, in a modern state, every citizen cannot be a legislator.

(3) In the modern state with representative a government, a citizen controls legislation, not by directly and personally taking part in law-making but by electing members of his own liking to the legislature. He does not rule, but chooses his rulers.

(4) Aristotle failed to fore-see the possibilities of representative government. In forms of government other than direct democracy, say, oligarchy, only a few participate in political functions and that for limited time only.

(5) Aristotle's definition of citizenship not only excluded large numbers of the population of the state but, since it implied membership of the legislative assembly and of the jury, could not be extended to the colonies or to subject distant cities. Not only did it endanger the safety of the state by creating a large disenfranchised and discontented class but it militated against the solidarity of the state and against the fusion of the conqueror and the conquered in one political system.

(6) It is true that Aristotle has a lofty conception of citizenship and its duties and, therefore, he excludes the leisureless working classes from citizenship but in doing this he is sacrificing the educative and ennobling effect of enjoying political privileges and performing political functions, incidental to citizenship, on the initially uninitiated and unqualified. Even a voice in the government in the shape of the right of election of the jurors and legislators has got its own civic, ethical and stabilizing value. A large indifferent and disenfranchised class is bound to tone down the civic excellence of the state.

(7) Aristotle's definition of citizenship cuts the society into two unequal halves and condemns the larger half to the position of a mere means to the welfare of the smaller half. It must be realised, however, that every human being has his own moral potentialities and is capable of a life worth living for itself. it is, therefore, the business of the state to secure rights, social and political, for its humblest as well as for its most cultivated members.

(8) Aristotle's theory is of value to us because it emphasize the obvious truth of the actual inequality of men but Aristotle goes too far in his division of society. No simple division of population into (1) the active and essential part of the state and (2) a mere means of the existence and welfare of the state (working classes) can do justice to the complex gradation, based on varying capacity, of members of the society.

(9) The Aristotelian idea of citizenship is very illiberal. If the end of the state is to serve the greatest good of the greatest number, it must be able to utilize the experience and potentialities as well as the differences of the largest part of its members. Again if citizenship is to be reserved only for a class of people who are rich enough not to have to work for their living, we might well be certain that the governing body, based on rich citizenship, would first and last think of passing legislation calculated to ensure the stability and permanence of the rule of its own class and would, therefore, identify the private interest of its own class with the public interest of the state. Laws would be passed to ensure for the ruling class large incomes.

It must be admitted, however, in justification of Aristotle's position that citizenship in his days connoted something much more than it nowadays does and did require leisure which the working classes did not enjoy. Aristotle realised this and, like the realist that he was, preferred the practicable to the ideally perfect. Like a realist, again, Aristotle held that a good citizen in a democracy had different virtues from a good citizen in an oligarchy. To Aristotle, judicial and deliberative, particularly the latter, functions represented the sovereignty of the state and, therefore, citizenship meant a direct share in the sovereignty of the state and not, as in the case of a modern state, a share in the election of a sovereign. The rights and duties of Aristotlean citizenship were large and, therefore, the number of citizens had to be correspondingly small.

13

Aristotle on Revolutions

In Book V (in some editions (in Book VII and VIII) of the 'Politics' Aristotle makes a masterly analysis of contemporary political evils and shows ripe political wisdom in suggesting preventives for them.

Frequent changes in the governments of the city-states, due to decadence and deterioration in political life made Aristotle to think and formulate his views on revolutions, their causes and preventive measures. Just as a physician examines the patient and suggests proper remedies for curing the disease, in the same way Aristotle ascertains the ills of the body-politic, examines the various causes of revolution and then suggest remedies for their prevention. In doing so he displays unique wisdom. His treatment of revolutions is divided into two parts. Part one is a practical manual of conduct advising oligarchs, democrats, aristocrats, monarchs and tyrants on how to keep themselves in power. Here he displays cool objectivity and sense of expediency which we find in the teachings of Machiavelli. Part two is a thesis on the philosophic basis of good and stable government. His treatment of the subject is historical and empirical.

Kinds of Revolution

According to Aristotle there are four kinds or degrees of revolution. A revolution may take the form of a change in the constitution of the state, such as making a change from oligarchy into democracy or from democracy into oligarchy or from either of them into constitutional government or aristocracy, and conversely. In the second kind the authors may have the constitution unchanged and be satisfied to seize political power into their own hands. In the third form a revolution may make an oligarchy more or less oligarchic, or a democracy more or less democratic. In the fourth form a revolution may be directed against any particular institution or set of persons in the state and may leave the form of government unchanged.

General Causes of Revolution

After describing these four kinds, Aristotle discusses the general causes of revolution.

Here he first tries to find out the source of revolution. To know it one must consider the temper of those who make, the motive behind the revolution and the causes and occasions of a revolution. The most general cause of revolution is the craving of men for equality. According to Aristotle men turn to civil strife when they have not their dues in proportion to their estimate of themselves. The masses always seek absolute equality, the oligarchic few are in favour of proportionate equality based on due consideration of wealth, ability and birth. This represents the state of mind of those who bring about revolutions. The objects of revolution are a gain and honour and equality, and the avoidance of loss and dishonour and inequality — absolute or proportional. The real reason is discrepancy between the actual political power and the actual political merit of the different sections of the population. The real spring of revolution is the innate desire in the average man to have equality of opportunities and rights. Stability of the state depends on the extent of the satisfaction of this craving.

Particular Causes of Revolution

After discussing the general cause of revolution. Aristotle discusses particular causes.

The first cause is insolence and avarice. According to Aristotle, "when the magistrates are insolent and grasping, they conspire against one another and also against the constitution from which they derive their power, making their gains either at the expense of individuals or of the public. Men who are themselves dishonoured and who see others obtaining honours rise in rebellion; the honour or dishonour when undeserved is unjust, and just when awarded according to merit."

The second cause of revolution is love of superiority. Aristotle says, "when one or more persons have a power which is too much for the state and the power of the government; this is a condition of affairs out of which there arises monarchy, or a family oligarchy." This state of affairs is disliked by the public and causes a revolution.

The third cause of revolution is fear. When men commit wrong and are afraid of punishment, they attempt to create a revolution to conceal their own misdeeds. Men also resort to revolution when they fear aggression from others.

The fourth cause of revolution is contempt. In oligarchies power resides in the hands of a few persons and the majority is left without it. These men of the majority revolt because they fell they are stronger.

Fifthly, disproportionate increase in any part of the state is the cause of revolution. This causes dissensions. Both the poor and the rich cannot tolerate preponderance of one another. So, Aristotle realized that stability depends on an equitable social and economic order. He was opposed to selfish class rule by either an excessively wealthy plutocracy or by a property-less proletariat. For him the best political community is of the middle class.

Other causes of revolution are election intrigues, carelessness shown in granting public offices to disloyal citizens, neglect on small changes which might become big later on, and discordance of elements in the state. Racial differences also become a cause of revolution. Sometimes trifling things become the cause of revolution. A marriage quarrel may spark off a revolution in democracies. Oligarchies are even thrown out by revolts due to their oppressive rule and mutual rivalry. Aristocracies fail as in them honours are restricted to a few people. Monarchies and tyrants fail because of their undignified behaviour. Foreign influence is also one of the causes.

Preventive for Revolutions

Aristotle like a good doctor made a number of practical remedies *i.e.,* suggestions as to the methods by which various forms of government may be successfully maintained and revolution prevented. Suggestions as to how to avoid revolutions are equally illuminating as their causes.

(1) He says the best way to prevent them is to preserve a friendly atmosphere, to counteract discontents, to act moderately, to avoid extremes, and "never wrong the common people in a matter of honour or the common people in a matter of money." Aristocracies and oligarchies may continue despite very imperfect constitutions simply through the wisdom of the rulers, who keep on good terms with their subjects.

(2) The ruler must be on the watch to effect the small changes in the constitution or the beginnings of a revolt and they should be nipped in the bud.

(3) The surest way to satisfy classes and masses is to throw the office open to all but without salaries.

(4) Another most essential thing is to inculcate the spirit of fairness and of reverence of law both on the part of the rulers and ruled. Lack of government and growth of arbitrariness change the good into bad forms. It is unwise for the rulers to rely on his capacity to deceive the people.

(5) Office must not be monopolised by a few families of a class of citizens *i.e.,* political power should not be allowed to concentrate in one or a few hands. Offices and honours should be awarded on considerations of the distributive justice. Various classes in the State, should be treated with consideration and equally associated with the government. No man or class of citizens should feel that they cannot hold political power. It should be open to merit.

(6) Patriotism of the people must be kept on the feverish pitch.

(7) Sound defence against foreign aggression makes a rulers popular.

(8) A close eye should be kept on changes in the distribution of wealth, since these have important political effects.

(9) The ruling group must remember their common interest and not give way to faction.

(10) For the sake of security of the State, Aristotle permits interference in the private life of the individual also. He says if marriages and friendships lead to revolt, they should be regulated by the State.

(11) Smaller offices should have long tenure and higher over a short tenure. In the words of Aristotle, the ruler should give moderate honour for a long time rather than great honour for a short time, for men are easily spoilt, not everyone can bear prosperity.

(12) The highest offices in the State should be given only on considerations of loyalty to the constitution, administrative capacity and integrity of character, but each citizen must have his due.

(13) No one must be allowed suddenly to rise in power, *i.e.,* access to power should be gradual and slow.

(14) The State should be so administered and so regulated by law that its magistrates or holders of offices cannot possible to get a chance to make money bribery or illegal gratification etc.

(15) Oligarchies and aristocracies should not relax their constitutions to be covered into democracies. The oligarchic and democratic spirit should not be pushed too far. The mean must be sought. Polity or a mixed form of government containing both oligarchic and democratic elements is the most natural and enduring and Aristotle's panacea against revolutions, as it is based on Popular will. Stability of State depends upon the satisfaction of the craving for equality. It is only with this form of government that equipoise and balance can be maintained. Stability can be maintained only by proportionate equality and by giving to each his own.

(16) The ruler or government should keep before the public the danger of foreign attack in case of internal revolt because excuse of external danger will overcome internal dissension. According to Aristotle, the ruler should invent terrors and keep distant dangers near so as to maintain loyalty. A feeling

of emergency must be maintained, what a close resemblance with Machiavelli.

(17) For the sake of gaining popularity and political stability its financial administration should be open to public security.

(18) "In democracies the property to the rich and in oligarchies the rights and dignity of the poor should be respected".

(19) Strangers and aliens should be kept away from the important political offices.

(20) The tyrant must chop off the inconvenient tall poppies. He must employ spies, especially female spies, to prevent quarrels, and keep people busy and poor. He must show zeal in ruling, own but with dignity and reserve. He must show favours personally but punish through others.

In conclusion, we can say that Aristotle's view on revolution as given in Politics have made the book a handbook of the statesmen for all times to come. As a matter of fact his theory anticipates Machiavelli. In his theory of revolution, he completely separates ethics from polities. His theory is, no doubt, one of the greatest contributions to political thought.

Distributive Justice

While dealing with revolutions Aristotle touches the subject of distributive justice as it plays an important role in the stability of state. Complete or absolute to Aristotle means virtue in action or excellence of character and it lies in conforming to law. But justice in narrower sense is particular justice and it is nothing but observing the rules of equality.

To be just is to assign a man his due *i.e.,* to share offices and honour in proportionate equality with others. This particular justice has two aspects, (1) corrective and (2) distributive justice. The corrective justice is mainly concerned with voluntary commercial transactions like sale, hire, furnishing of security, etc. and other things like aggression on property, life, honour and freedom. Distributive justice, on the other contributions to the society in the form of wealth or virtue. It is mainly concerned with political rights. Every form of government has its own standard of distributive justice for instance, "in a democracy, the standard of worth is free birth, in an oligarchy it is riches, in aristocracy of birth it is descent while in true aristocracy it is virtue." Aristotle says that a virtuous state discards both the democratic and oligarchic citizen, has moral wisdom, military strength and property and efficiency in some particular direction. Distributive justice is nothing but proportionate equality and it lessens frictions and confusion by countering in equality of the equals or the equality of the unequals. This justice gives offices, honours and other reward according to the social performance and contribution to the society and at the same time prevents encroachment by one member upon the sphere of another.

Aristotle says that office and honours should not be restricted only to the virtuous few but should be open to all the citizens. He feels that people collectively make an important contribution to the State and must be proportionately rewarded. He believes in the collective wisdom of the people in electing and judging the magistrates. Every class has something to contribute and thereby entitles itself to some share in political power. A stable to be stable, needs more supporters than enemies. He wanted to reconcile principle of democracy with his philosophy of justice and thereby evolve a liberal constitution to today. But this concept of distributive justice of Aristotle cannot apply to modern big States against city State of his times. Moreover, our notion of distributive justice is based on duties rather than rights, particularly the duty of paying proportionate taxes to the State. Now the office and honour must also go to merit.

On Tyrants

Discussion on revolution led Aristotle to deal with tyrants also. He relates what methods do the tyrants use to maintain their power, how they are usually overthrown and what preventives they can use to preserve their regimes. Here Aristotle keeps aside his ethical considerations and separates politics from ethics, and thereby seems to be modern.

A tyrant of Aristotle's days was an enlightened despot. According to Aristotle, a tyrant maintains himself in power on the basis of espionage especially through women spies. He always diverts the attention of his subjects from internal maladministration and unjustice to foreign wars successfully waged and to glories to victories won. He keeps patriotism of the people on the highest pitch. He sows quarrels among the various classes of his subjects, and impoverishes them for the support of his guards: the people, if kept hard at work, are prevented from conspiring. He lops off those who are too high and takes measures to prevent people from knowing one another well, and prohibit intelligent discussion. He tries totally to destroy the intellectual life of the citizens to render them incapable of political speculation which is dangerous for a tyrant.

A tyrant is bond of bad men and dislikes anyone of independence; but women and slaves supports them, for under him they have a good time. While destroying the intellectual life of his subjects he should try to improve their material well being. He should dispense justice to rich and poor alike. He should show favour himself but punishes through others. The flatter friend of tyant should remain austere and wide awake. He should appear to do everything for the public good and show sympathy and concern for the people and thereby gain the goodwill of the people. He should refrain from taking material gain for himself from his power and position. He should be particularly earnest in the service of the Good and in promotion of fine arts.

He cloaks his feeling and actions and self confidence behind the interests of State. In Aristotles' own words, "Let his disposition be virtuous, or at least half virtuous, and if he must be wicked, let him be half wicked only." The whole picture is a masterly performance, outclassing Machiavelli on his ground and valid in any age.

14

Aristotle on Law and Sovereignty

Aristotle on Law

Like Plato and Socrates, Aristotle also gives importance to the laws of society. He interprets law as the great preventive and restraining force of a community. He defines law as the sum of all the spiritual limits under which man's actions must proceed. He describes law as a dispassionate reason. He prefers the rule of law to the rule of men. The aim of law is the same as that of the state.

It is to promote good life. Law is moral code as it determines the morality and spirituality of community. It is this character of law which makes it sovereign. His pure states were law-governed states in which the rulers were essentially administrators and guardians of law. Aristotle's law was not only dispassionate reason, it was also social experience, wisdom and social conscience. It was enacted by desire. True law possesses the divine and rational elements. Laws can be changed if newer and better are to be found. But changes should be very few, for the habit of lightly changing the laws is an evil. Aristotle regards law as natural. As it is identical with the eternal and immutable laws of morality, it is natural. It is as natural as family, property and slavery. It is also as moral as they are.

Aristotle on Sovereignty

Aristotle on Sovereignty was not known to the Greeks. The word 'Sovereignty' is derived from the Latin word 'Supernas', meaning supreme. The modern concept of sovereignty assigns the sovereign state complete internal supremacy and absolute external independence. The Greek had no definite and clear ideas of sovereignty even though the Greek city-states were internally supreme and externally independent. Though Aristotle's classification of states on the basis of the location of supreme power in the hands of one, few or many did point in the direction of sovereignty, yet Aristotle had little idea of what we consider sovereignty to be. His conception rules out the concept of sovereignty which involves supremacy over law, for any authority over law is abrogation of law. To Aristotle, law itself is sovereign and there is no sovereign besides law. There is no constitution where law is not supreme.

Modern sovereignty is a legalistic conception, the outgrowth of the ideas of Roman Law and their application to modern nation states. Aristotle refers to the 'supreme power' in the state and discusses the problem of its location. It is tempting to identify this supreme power with the modern sovereigns. It must be realised, however, that Aristotle's discussion of supremacy or supreme power is nothing but an 'ethico-political appraisal' of the relations of the political koimonia (state) with other smaller associations of men. He does not refer to supremacy as something defined in terms of law but to an actual supremacy possessed by an economic or social class and ensured, not by legal but by physical sanctions.

The foregoing conclusion *viz*, that to Aristotle supremacy meant *de facto* and not *de jure* supremacy, is borne out if we consider his views on Revolution. A revolution in the modern times, involves the subversion of the legal basis of the state more than anything else. To Aristotle, a revolution represented a political change rather than a 'legal' one. It involved reversal not so much of legal, as of ethical, social and economic standards.

While dealing with the various forms of government and state, Aristotle refers to the sovereignty of law. Sovereignty of law, however, does not mean the legal sovereign. It only means that the true relation between law and the government is that the law is master and the governments is agent. Aristotle holds that 'where laws have no authority, there is no constitution. The law ought to be supreme over all and the rulers should judge of particulars.' The closest Aristotelian counterpart of a modern legal sovereign is a body of citizens performing judicial but particularly deliberative functions which are the essential functions of the state. The deliberative is supreme over the constitution and as its determinant it is sovereign. In spite of this comparative identification of sovereignty of with judicial but particularly deliberative functions and parts of the state, Aristotle's conception of sovereignty falls far short of the modern concept of sovereignty.

Supremacy — Justification

In the second chapter of his Book I Aristotle attacks the problem of the nature of the state and the rightfulness of its authority. As a Greek, he finds justification of domestic and political life and, therefore, of state and its authority in the nature of man which requires the household and the state for his highest well-being. The household may suffice for the bare existence of the individual and for his elementary needs, but an individual needs higher social entity than a family to meet the needs of a fuller life. Man is by nature a political being. The very faculties which make him the highest being of nature require, for their exercise, that environment which the state alone that can provide and ensure. In the state alone the individual becomes a man. To attain a happy and rich life, men want the individual becomes rich variety of interests. It is the state alone that can organise and maintain this rich variety of interests through a complex social order. The state is necessary to man because (1) it alone can bring about a diversity of interests and variety of life essential to man; (2) through civic training and participation in public affairs, the state enables the individual to lead a 'good' life and (3) the state renders possible an orderly and peaceful existence. The performance of this threefold service, however, depends upon the supremacy of the state over all causes, interests and elements in the state. The state must be supreme to be able to regulate.

Location of Supreme Power in the State

Aristotle poses the question as to where supremacy in the state should reside in the multitude, the wealthy, the noble born or the good; in one man, few or many. Any one of these alternatives seems to involve disagreeable consequences. If the supreme power is in the hands of the multitudinous poor, the poor may exercise their authority to rob the rich which will be injustice. The wealthy few, invested with supreme power, may adopt class-legislation the harm of the poor. Supreme power in the hands of the good means dishonour to others. The many, if taken collectively, may be better than the few good. After a good deal of discussion, Aristotle fixes on polity as representing the best type of government, and, by preference, places his supreme power in the hands of the middle class.

To Aristotle, the location of supreme power in the state is a very important consideration. In fact, the very identity of the state depends on this. A revolution in the state which does not involve a change in the location of supreme power in the state is not a revolution but a mere change of government officers. If, on the other hand, supreme power was shifted from one class to another, the state itself was changed.

Legal and Popular Sovereignty

The modern view of sovereignty based on Austinian conception of legal sovereignty is that sovereignty is indivisible and it must, in the final analysis, be possessed by some organ of the state. Such a view is born of the doctrine that identifies sovereignty with the supreme law-making power, particularly the power of enacting constitutional laws. Aristotle, like contemporary Greeks, did not consider the enactment of laws as the highest function of the state and would not completely identify sovereignty with the law-making organ in the state. Modern sovereignty, moreover, does not consider a mixed form of government as a logical possibility, whereas Aristotle's ideal polity is of mixed form.

While the democratic preferences of Aristotle are fairly well pronounced, he cannot be said to be a believer in what is known in modern times as the doctrine of popular sovereignty with its concomitants, *viz.*, natural equality of all men, majority rule and rights of the state being based on the consent of the governed. On the contrary, to Aristotle, the authority and sovereignty of the state is based on natural law. Men are fundamentally unequal and nature provides for the sovereignty of the state by ordaining certain type of relationship between the ruler and the ruled and the master and the slave. If Aristotle allows popular participation in assemblies and courts of laws, it is because of expediency and to avoid discontent and revolution.

Aristotle hold that the supreme power in the state must be subject to laws. The ruling authority — one, few or many — must act in consonance with the laws and should have supreme authority only in those matters on which the laws do not pronounce exactly. Aristotle, however, makes an exception, as did Plato, in favour of superior, however, make an excellent merit like that of a philosopher-ruler. While Aristotle assigned ultimate sovereignty of laws, it was not without qualms of political conscience. He knew that laws were relative to the polity in which they existed, those of *pure* politics being good and just and of perverted politics being bad and unjust.

Limitation on Supreme Power — Absolute State

Aristotle held that the sphere of activity and, therefore, the extent of the authority of the state was indicated by the state. The end of the state was to make men virtuous and happy and, therefore, there could be no limit to the legitimate exercise of state authority. Of course, in an ideal state, the supreme authority will not impose unnatural restrictions like communism of Plato on the free and full development of the individual and will create environment congenial to such development. But Aristotle allowed this concession to the individual on grounds of expediency. "As little as Plato does Aristotle have (the idea) that there belongs by nature to individuals certain sphere of freedom upon which it is never legitimate for the political power to trespass. To him, as to all the ancients, the absolutism of the state is unquestioned. Men are to be made virtuous and happy, no matter what degree of interference in their lives on the part of the state this implies. The individual is not conceived of as having any rights, or indeed as being a person at all outside of the civil body."

15

Aristotle As Scientist

Aristotle was a versatile genius. His knowledge was encyclopaedic and he wrote on ethics and metaphysics, art and poetry, economics and politics, physics and mechanics, physiology and medicine, on astronomy and logic. The great importance of Aristotle, in the realm of political philosophy, lies in the fact that he gave to politics the character of an independent science. It is no exaggeration to say that real political science in the west begins, not with Plato, but with Aristotle, who laid the foundations of the subject with his rate political insight and systematic treatment. Some of the political observations and theories of Aristotle are very shrewd, apply to all forms of social and political life and show the universal and the permanent in Aristotle.

Aristotle's political sanity makes him a safe guide for future generations.

Aristotle puts up an exalted civic ideal of a state government by reason and law in which all free-born are allowed some participation in civic affairs. The end of the state is not merely life but virtuous and happy life. Aristotle pleads for extension not of area and population but of virtue and happiness in the State.

The actual information contained in the Politics of Aristotle regarding conditions of Greek civic life is invaluable though that is counter-balanced by the fact that Aristotle's writings have reference to the Hellenic city-state and ignore other forms of government or non-Hellenic forms of social and economic organisation.

Aristotle had none of the high enthusiasm or poetic imagination of Plato. He shows impatience of Plato's idealism and lack of touch with reality. He regarded himself as a scientist. At the same time, he is regarded as a propounder of new philosophy.

It is true that Aristotle's reasoning is logical and scientific and is based on facts collected from existing constitutions and institutions, Hellenic or barbarian, with meticulous care and rate observation. Like a true scientist, Aristotle had the art of distinguishing between the essential and the non-essential and between categories. Whereas with Plato, Politics was a handmaid of Ethics, Aristotle separated the two and treated them systematically in two different treatises, *i.e.*, his Politics and the Nicomachean Ethics.

Plato viewed society dynamically and was lost in the mysticism of the universal, the Eternal and the Absolute. Aristotle looked at Society statistically and worked empirically. It has been aptly said that Plato, tired of degenerate practical politics of contemporary Athens, turned to the Ideal State while Aristotle tired by Ideal State portrayed by Plato and others, turned to practical politics based on empirical methods. From this we know the poet in Plato and the scientist in Aristotle.

Aristotle's scientific nature of the political observation and speculation is evident not only from his empirical study of the existing material but also from his method of approach to the subject. With analytical precision, characteristic of him Aristotle classifies constitutions, distinguishes between State and Government, treats properly of the morphology and pathology of the state, discussing minutely the causes and course of Revolution.

Thus, from above it is very obvious that Aristotle gave to politics the character of an independent science.

16

The Ideal and the Best State of Aristotle

In the later writings the consuming fire of Plato's early enthusiasm gave way to sober realities, according to Barker. Hence, grudgingly and half-heartedly he states a second type of best State. In the case of Aristotle, his approach was more empirical and descriptive. The whole science of politics, according to the new idea, included the knowledge of both political good and also of political mechanics. This is a wider conception of Aristotle. Salime calls this enlargement of the definition of political philosophy as Aristotle's most characteristics conception. This widening of the scope of politics in the writings of Aristotle naturally made him compromise the ideals of Platonic State with these of practical realities. In the case of Plato, it was a forced constitution due to frailty of human nature and in the case of Aristotle, it was a full fledged conviction. That is to say, the ghost of Plato made Aristotle a fully captive.

Law

There is a striking similarity between the second Best State of Plato and the Ideal State of Aristotle with regards to law, not as a make-shift but as a necessary condition for moralised and civilised life. He made law supreme in his State. He regards it as the wisdom of the ages. He applies it from marriage to the burial of the dead.

Aristotle calls that man when perfected is best of animals, but when separated from law and justice, he is the worst of all. It is possible, says Aristotle that in making a law. The collective wisdom of the people is superior to that of even the wisest law-giver. Above the sovereignty of the people, however, Aristotle, like a true Greek, places the sovereignty of law. The supremacy of law is accepted by him as a mark of good state and not merely as an unfortunate necessity or as a concession to human frailty. According to Salime, "even the wisest ruler cannot dispense with law, because the law has an impersonal quality which no man however good, can attain." The law is "reason unaffected by desire."

Communism

Aristotle vehemently attacks the Platonic conception of communism as stated in the 'Republic'. But he is one with communism as diluted in the 'Statesman' and 'the Laws'.

In his later works, Plato speaks of common ownership of land. At the same time he recognises ownership of private property. This thing is totally given up by Aristotle in his Ideal State. But Aristotle, like Plato would like that there should be one common meal table because taking of meals together would promote stability and unity of the State. Aristotle would divide the land into two parts. "One public and other private....half the public land being appropriated to the service of the good, the other used to defray the cost of common meals.."

Aristotle dislikes the community of wives as given in Plato's Republic; but he agrees with Plato in allowing women to have education. One thing, about which Aristotle is not clear is whether women should be allowed an equal opportunity to take up public offices or not.

Ethics

Both Plato and Aristotle gave greater place to Ethics. Aristotle's political ideal was quite one with Plato's in setting upon ethical purpose as the chief end of the State. The real purpose of the State ought to include the moral improvement of its citizens, because it ought to be an association of men living together to achieve the best possible life. This is the 'idea' or meaning of a State. The State alone is "self-sufficing" in the sense that it alone provides all the conditions within which the highest type of moral development can take place.

The only difference between Plato's and Aristotle's treatment is that the former describes his true State as law-abiding and the latter describes it as governing for the general good. This is only minor as both of them believe that morality should cover the activities of the State.

Education

Both Plato and Aristotle give a prominent place for education. No doubt in both cases it occupies an eminent and excellent place. The Chief function, according to them, of the State should be a scientific course of education designed to cultivate moral, intellectual and physical excellence in its citizens for the due performance of their civic functions. A system of uniform compulsory and public education is the first necessity of an Ideal State.

Aristotle's educational scheme generally resembles that of Plato. It is meant for leisured citizens. It aims at moral and mental culture rather than at practical or professional utility, lays stress on physical training and attaches to music and character-building virtues. He also lays emphasis on gymnastics and music; the former helps in bringing beauty, grace and symmetry in the body and the latter in producing a sound-mind.

In the case of Plato, a good deal of attention was paid in describing at length about education. In the case of Aristotle, the details are lacking; but Salime says, it may be due to the reason that he was not able to furnish the necessary details due to his early death.

The discussion of Aristotle on liberal education and his contempt for the useful is little higher than Plato. Aristotle agrees that children have to be taught some useful things, "but to be always seeking after the useful does not become exalted." There is an apparent touch of romanticism and idealising of an aristocratic way of life.

City-States in Mind

Both of them conceive their States in the setting of Greek City-States. When Plato spoke of his second best State and Aristotle of his ideal state, they were having only the city-States in mind and not any bigger unit. Even Aristotle sailed to see that the future lay for bigger States, and not,for the city-states as shown by the conquests of his disciple, Alexander the Great.

Similarity in Details

There is a lot of similarity in the details as given by Plato for his second best State and the ideal state of Aristotle. Plato speaks how that his second best State cannot be located on the sea-shore. It must be agricultural and it should have all the machinery of a democracy like the Assembly, The Council of Elders, Magistrates etc. While accepting all these things, Aristotle does not fall in line with the first detail *viz*. the State should be only inland.

Democracy

In his 'Statesman' and the 'Laws', Plato states a mixed State consisting of the principles of monarchy and democracy, *i.e.*, he preserved the spirit of the philosopher. Kings as absolute and making it function through a democratic apparatus. In the case of Aristotle, the belief in democracy is much greater because the State exists for the good of the citizens. To Aristotle constitutional rule means that it is in the public or general interest. It is carried out by general regulations and not by arbitrary decrees as it is the government of willing subjects. The constitutional ruler rules by consent and is quite different from a dictator. This is a great advance on Platonic thought, but unfortunately it was not examined systematically and thoroughly.

Classifications of States

Aristotle fully copied the division of States into six categories of Plato. The only difference being that Plato describes his true States as law-abiding and Aristotle as existing for the general good.

The principle of separation of powers was also brought out and proper organisation and duties of executive, legislative and judicial reigns were examined.

The proper apportionment of political power is fundamental to the security of the State according to the views of Plato and Aristotle.

Slavery

Both Plato and Aristotle cannot conceive of a state without being based on the system of slavery. Their States cannot function without leisured citizens who can get leisure only by employing slaves for their household and their duties regarding their livelihood.

It is better and fitter if we conclude this Chapter in the words of Salime, *i.e.*, "Ideals must not exist like Plato's pattern in the heavens but as forces working in and through agencies by no means ideal." To put it in a nutshell Aristotle's States annoted, underlined and confirmed Plato's second Best State.

17

The Hellenic and Universal in Aristotle

The political philosophy of Aristotle is primarily based on a detailed and systematic study of the Hellenic, historical and contemporary constitutions, social and political institutions and practices. His *Politics* represents an attempt to rationalize existing Hellenic institutions and suggest improvements therein. His main ideas — the naturalness and justice of slavery, the superiority of the Greeks over other people and races, and the city-state representing the best form of political organisation and the necessity of freedom from economic worries — are Hellenic in their outlook and character.

The Hellenic in Aristotle, Prof. Dunning says "The foregoing sketch of Aristotle's work should at least suggest the importance of the Hellenic elements in his political philosophy. His historical research went far beyond the confines of Hellas, out the system which he framed was determined in its most essential characteristics by the conditions that prevailed within those continues." The Hellenic elements in Aristotle's political philosophy are immensely impressive.

His insistence on a state-controlled and a state-directed system of education, and on the necessity of educating citizens in the laws and constitution of the city-state are Spartan in character. His attitude towards commerce and usury is Hellenic. His subordination of all private and personal interest, as well as human conduct to the authority of law, is Hellenic in character. There is no doubt that most of the ideas of Aristotle have lost this significance in the course of the ages but, according to Dunning, "But when we look further into his philosophy, beneath the general outlines determined by these Hellenic dogmas, we find a long series of principles which are as ultimate as human nature itself, and which, in almost the exact shape in which Aristotle formulated them, are features of political science at the present day."

According to Murray, "Perhaps the most striking feature of the *Politics* is the extent to which, notwithstanding the very different political and social environment of ancient Greece, Aristotle succeeded in formulating the principles which are now generally accepted as the moral basis of democratic government."

Thus, we find in the features of Aristotle's philosophy a lot of universalism.

The first such principle is Aristotle's conception of the sovereignty of law. This principle, 'as a rule of law', has been universally accepted today by almost all states believing in democracy and incorporated by them in their constitutional practices. The law, represented as dispassionate reason and embodying experience of the past was also accepted by the Middle Ages. Dicey's rule of Law is essentially based on Aristotle's doctrine of the sovereignty of law. Dunning says, "In the course of ages most of these ideas either have passed entirely out of consideration or have been so modified as to lose the significance which Aristotle attaches them."

His doctrine of the golden mean is a pre-cursor of the modern notion of political checks and balances as accepted in the U.S.A. In the words of Catlin, "After Confucius, Aristotle is the supreme Apostle of common sense and of the Golden Means. The practical nature of his philosophy is not virtue but it is a necessity to virtue. Men cannot live on poetry alone, but they need satiating, their gastric desires too." The doctrine finds an echo in the 19th century and in German National Socialism.

The permanent and universal side of Aristotle's philosophy is especially reflected in the importance he attaches to economic influence in political organization and activity. According to Dunning, "from this is derived that doctrine which has been so impressively confirmed by later history, that stability and prosperity are most to be found where extremes of wealth and poverty and unknown and the middle class is the strongest."

His stress on the value of public opinion is refreshingly modern *i.e.*, Aristotle is of the opinion that the work of officials is best judged by the masses and not by the exports.

Holding that the aggregate virtue and political wisdom of the mass of a people as greater than that of any part of it. Aristotle allowed the people, as a whole, the function of final judgement on official action.

His ideas on the establishment of social justice, based on the doctrine of proportionate equality, have become the slogans of all advocates of socialism and economic democracy.

The thesis of the welfare state is derived from Aristotle's theory of the state. He holds that "individual is prior to the state" which shows that he is in fact an individualist.

Finally, in the importance that he attaches to the individual, Aristotle has often been called, the father of modern individualism. His ideas on family and property as natural and necessary institutions for man have received widest support. His views on the sphere of state activity show his sane individualism. His statement that the "state comes into existence for the sake of life but it continues to exist for the sake of good life" is a very important statement supporting the cause of the individual, and explaining the duties of the state. He does not treat the state as an end but a means to an end, which is the highest good of its members. The state must allow an individual to lead a full life and for that reason it must give him considerable amount of freedom. He refuses to sacrifice the individual arise from the state and are conditioned by the duty of the state of make men happy and virtuous.

Aristotle is the philosopher of common sense, of the middle class and of the golden mean. He is not a proletarian democrat. He is a liberal opposed to all forms of dictatorship. He has no faith in the class rule of either Plato or Marx.

No doubt, Aristotle is, therefore, regarded as father of political science and the father of modern individualisation.

18

Aristotle as a Conservative, Democrat and Socialist

The philosophy of Aristotle exhibits a best amount of knowledge as he tested the ideal of Plato with actual practicalities. As he was an empirical philosopher, he widened the scope of politics and thereby enriched it. He was called 'The Philosopher' throughout the Middle Ages and he was known to have been called by Dante as the 'Master of Them That Knew', that is to say, it was he who inspired and attracted most of the thinkers during the medieval period whereas his master Plato was kept in the cold storage. The extensive knowledge exhibited by Aristotle proved a fertile field for many new ideas. These ideas called conservatism, democracy and socialism are to be found in his philosophy in a raw material form. Aristotle was never a conscious conservative, democrat or socialist in our modern sense. What all happened was extensive discourses enable us to find the seeds or the three doctrines in his writings.

As Conservative

He can be called conservative for the reason that he said that character depends upon the way a man is brought up. This meant the rituals, traditions, customs and usages do shape the character of man. Naturally Aristotle showed great regard for these things in Greece of those times. He nationalises existing institution. He rules out traders and artisans from citizenship. Any person who holds the existing order to be respected is conservative and hence Aristotle is called conservative.

Secondly, the way in which he regarded the slave system of those times show him to be a conservative but not a radical. He said that just as subjection is good for beast, so also is the slave system for some people. The brawn must serve the brain.

All the same, one cannot accuse Aristotle of cruelty or harshness towards them. It is because he himself married from slave class and finally in his will, he provided for the freedom of the slaves his household. In short, he neither bettered not worsened the situation. What all he did was by trying to explain the slave system by the reasons of heredity that cannonized it.

Thirdly, his whole philosophy and outlook was conceived in the Polis. His vision never widened beyond the limits of the city-states. He considered it to be central and congenial to the attainment of good life which is the end of the State.

Fourthly, he trusted more in the law than any other previous thinker. The law is sovereign in the State. In the Grecian life, law is regarded with great sacredness and respect. By making law to be the sovereign of the State, what he did was once again placing the existing belief on a high alter.

Lastly, Catlin considers that his distrust of amateur and advertiser is a conservative outlook. That it to say, a mere expert in the art of statesmanship and statecraft is no success in the modern world. Catlin says, 'the successful ruler must be a pressman assisted by Goehbles.'

As Democrat

Nextly, he can also be called a democrat for the reason that the central theme of his philosophy is, "on universals exist apart from the individuals," as stated by him in his metaphysics. This means, things must proceed from individual human beings but not from abstract principles. This is equal to the democratic principles which put value on each individual. He was in favour of individual liberty for development.

Secondly, it may be doubted how can he be called a champion of democracy when he totally disregarded a part of the population as not being fit for citizenship.

Still he is democrat in the limited sense for the reason that all the citizens are on equal level unlike the people of Plato who considered the majority of the citizens to be the meek and dumb herd.

Thirdly, his opinion of citizenship is that each citizen should have a share in the State activities. It is only those, who participate in the administrative and judicial organisation of the State, are to be called the citizens, according to him. The modern democracy means the equal participation of all the citizens in the activities of the State and so also in the opinion of Aristotle.

Fourthly, he believes in collective wisdom. He always had a distrust in the superiority and correctness of a few individuals. He often repeated that when large number of people are gathered together and when different points of view are expressed, there is scope for great wisdom. In this connection it may be mentioned how Aristotle did not believe in the full participation of women also in the political field. This cannot be a point against his democratic tendency for the reason that it was only in the twentieth century that most of the democratic States placed women on a footing of equality, and a democratic country like Switzerland has not given political right to women even till this day.

Though he is not a proletarian democrat and does not believe in mob democracy, but he is liberal democrat opposed to all forms of dictatorship even of philosophers. Nor does he believe in the class-rule of Plato or Marx. He realises the soundness of the political judgement of the common man. "It is possible that the many of which each individual is not a man of talent, are still collectively superior to the few best persons."

As Socialist

Nextly, he can also be called a socialist for the reason that he thought there should be an equitable distribution of wealth but not an equal distribution of wealth. As a matter of fact, he condemned the type of economy advocated by Plato but he too is for a regulated type of economy. He says that there should be a private ownership of property but it should be shared in common.

Secondly, in his best practicable State, the middle class formed the backbone. It is they who are neither too rich nor too poor. So also the case of modern socialism which banks mostly on the middle class who are neither capitalists not communists.

Thirdly, he was also against 'interest lending; which he thought would lead to the concentration of wealth in a few hands. The growth of modern capitalism is the direct result of banking and credit organisations. So naturally when he was against leading on interest, we can safely call him a socialist in ideas.

Fourthly, he also advocated that strong measure should be taken against speculation. It is one of the methods which often disturbs the economic equilibrium. So when he thought that it must be suppressed, he reviewed that State just like a socialist which wants the state so be an umpire between the conflicting economic interests of the State.

Lastly he believed that in human Society, extremes of wealth and poverty are the main sources of evil, and there can be no peace in the state where population is divided into two classes of too rich and too poor. They will be hostile to each other. This is class war. There can be no real friendship between the classes and friendship is the essential principle of all associations.

Thus, it can be very easily proved that Aristotle is somewhat a conservative, a democrat and a socialist. No one can say that he was an advocate and a champion of these doctrines. They exist only in embryo form in his political philosophy. Scholars even found him to be a Fascist as his philosophy exhibited a wide erudition in his detailed discussion. He was a Biologist, Mathematician, Metaphysician and even a Humourist who is supposed to have said that a beautiful lady needs no introductory letter.

19

Aristotle's Ideals and Actuals

Aristotle never completed his ideal State for which be gave introduction in his Book III. It is because of the reason that the ideals were sunk in the mid stream of realities. Hence, the remark of Salime, "what all he wrote was a book not on an Ideal State but of the ideals of the State." This fact in Aristotle's philosophy is due to the reason that he was more empirical and descriptive. He did not have the bold sweep and courage of Plato to destroy all that stood in his way. He is more cautious and moderate. To put it in other words, he is more of a reformatory than a revolutionary. Moreover, this new life he took up did not lead to any barren results. This revolt on Plato was fruitful in the sense that he opened new world in political science, which became much wider in extent and scope.

The conflict between the ideal and the actual can be first found with regard to law. Alongwith Plato, he agrees that law is not a make-shift but the wisdom of the ages. It means that law must be supreme and cannot be changed. But according to Aristotle, law is relative to the constitution and a bad state will have bad laws when he came to analyse actuals.

Secondly, He agrees with Plato that wisdom and virtue can have an absolute claim. But he says while dealing with the actuals that virtue and wisdom may be changed according to social and economic relations of a State. This means that there is conflict between the wisdom which he believed an ideal in Book III and wisdom that he found in Books VII and VIII.

Moreover, he took wholesale the six fold classification of Plato, but when he came to speak of actual States, he tells us of more varieties. He thinks that Monarchy and Aristocracy alone can be regarded as Ideal States, but when turns to the examination of existing monarchies, he drops the idea of the Ideal State. There he speaks about the kingship of Sparta, Persia and Oriental Monarchy.

This collision between the Ideal State of Book III and actuals that he came across is due to the reason that he was a disciple of Plato. The Ideal State of Plato took such a firm hold in the mind of Aristotle that he was able to free himself from it only at a later stage. The greatness of Aristotle consists in the fact that an ideal can be never an actual, that is to say, his ideal was softened and moderated by the hard facts of realities. In the words of Salime, "He is more soberer than Plato though not an original genius."

This compromise of the ideals with the actuals resulted in profound discoveries. In this beginning he spoke of the constitution as a kind of life and government as the expression of the kind of life it is to develop, but when he met realities, he said that constitution is a body of rules and regulation by which a State is to be managed. The second rich result was that he divorced politics from ethics or morals, thereby destroying the work of Socrates and Plato both. He says that politics must enable the State to make statesmen perfect in the art of government. That is why, he goes to the ridiculous extent of even giving advice to the tyrant as to how he can regulate and maintain his tyranny.

The important role played by actuals in the philosophy of Aristotle was described by Popper in a funny manner. In his interesting analysis of Aristotle his second volume of "Open Society and its Enemies" feels that Aristotle's interpretations of good society were coloured by his necessity for making a living as a popular teacher and by drafting and selling constitutions for various city-states of his times. This is because of the fact that he was poor whereas it was never a necessity with Plato who was aristocrate.

Thus, Aristotle's Ideal State became incompatible with the actualities. It brought a rich harvest to Political Science. The new conceptions like the constitution, divorcing of politics from ethics, the influence played by social and economic factors and his recognition of the fact that ideal is an ideal, are of far reaching consequences to the Political Science, as they came to be developed as various manifestations of Political Science. In short, the incompatibility of his ideal and his actuals did not drag his contribution into the quagmire but to new paths.

20

The Influence of Aristotle's Philosophy

It is because of its universality that Aristotle's thought wielded tremendous influence in ancient, medieval and modern ages. He influenced the imperialist as well as the ecelesiastical thinkers of the middle ages, St. Aquinas, Marsiglio of Padua, Dante and Machiavelli — all are indebted to him for their thoughts, Bodin, Harringten, Montesquieu have borrowed much from him. He has appealed to Hegel and advocates of the Historical and Sociological schools of thought. Dunning writes, "In systems so diverse as those of military Rome, of the theological Middle Age, and of the materialistic modern era, the essential features of political organization and activity explicable, and actually explained are on the lines of Aristotelian analysis."

It is no exaggeration to say that practical political philosophy in the West began with Aristotle. While Plato soared in the heights and aimed at the ideal, Aristotle's objective was not the ideal but the best that could be attained. By his keen and practical political insight and systematic treatment of the subject he laid the foundations of real Political Science. Though, like Plato, he too combined the ethical and political, he always gave primary importance to the political. He was more individualistic than Plato. He is analytical, logical and realistic and his theories represent definite and clear-cut dogmas.

In his 'History of Classical Scholarship' Sandys observes : "No single thinker, not even Plato has had as much impact as Aristotle on intellectual and institutional history of later centuries."

Max Learner says, "The religious systems were philosophically uncreated and needed a logic and critical framework and these Aristotle made available."

Barker remarks, "It is perhaps in Marsiglio of Padua that Aristotle's influence is most remarkable." Marsiglio of Padua was thus greatly influenced by Aristotle.

It goes without saying that in the West, the practical political philosophy began with Aristotle.

He may be rightly called the scientist of politics because of his empirical study and his method of approach to a problem. He collects his data with great care and categorises and defines them and draws rationalistic conclusion there from.

His philosophy has wielded tremendous influence in all ages. If St. Thomas Acquinas was Aristotelian in his method and in much of the content of his thoughts, Marsiglio and Dante show in no less way traces of Aristotelian thought. Machiavelli's Prince is said to be a commentary on the Aristotelian theory of revolution.

Even the modern age is not free from his influence. Montesquieu, both in the form and content of his thoughts, is indebted to Aristotle. His theory of separation of power was certainly inspired by Aristotle. Even the Hegelian theory of the constitution of a country representing the expression of the self-consciousness of the state is, in some measure, in agreement with Aristotle's view on the subject. The close relationship between economics and politics established by Karl Marx is also traceable to Aristotle.

Modern historical and sociological schools of thought owe much to Aristotle. Aristotle is also a source of inspiration to modern progressive conservatism, and to the critics of egalitarian democracy. His Politics still remains one of the greatest classics of political science. Barker remarks, "Aristotle taught St. Thomas; through St. Thomas he taught Catholic Europe; through St. Thomas he also taught Richard Hooker, who drew from the origin of the theory of law and government.....The judicious Hooker was in turn one of the masters of Locke....Theory of Locke descended in turn to Burke.....There is not only an analogy.....between the climate of Aristotle's politics and the climate of English political thought in the seventeenth and eighteenth countries. There is also some measure of affiliation."

With regard to his influence, Doyle writes "Aristotle gave to the world definitions of political terms which it has not yet had to supersede. Moreover, his ideal of mixed government and his acute analysis of the adjustments necessary between the component parts of the body-politic were models to succeeding generations. Aristotle propounded scientifically, with fruitful illustrations from contemporary sources, the nature of government, its forms and variations and the essential laws controlling its corporate life. On the foundations laid by these two thinkers (Plato and Aristotle) many subsequent generations have built and rebuilt their theories of Politics." Dante in his 'De Monarchia' refers to 'Politics' again and again. Machiavelli too was greatly influenced by Aristotle.

Gettell writes about Aristotle thus : "Aristotle was practical, logical and systematic. He reasoned inductively from a comparative and scientific study of the governmental systems that were actually in existence. His discussions, based on history and observation, are clear and precise, with relatively little poetic or allegorical embellishment. He separated political and ethical concepts and thus made possible an independent science of politics." Professor Gettell further writes, "Aristotle's contribution to Political thought is important because of the actual information it gives concerning the conditions of Greek constitutional life. It established a logical method of political inquiry and made possible a distinct science of the state. While based on conditions in the Greek world, Aristotle's work contained many profound generalizations applicable to political life in all times and places."

The 'Politics' of Aristotle is one of the greatest classics on political science. Zeller says, "The Politics of Aristotle is the richest treasure that has come down to us from antiquity, it is the greatest contribution to the field of political science that we possess."

Finally, we close this chapter with the observation of Maxey who wrote, "Everyone", said the poet Coleridge, "is born either a Platonist or an Aristotelian, which might be supplemented by the almost equally true observation that everyone maybe at one time a Platonist and at another an Aristotelian. So universal are the qualities of these two giants of Greek philosophy, and so perfectly do they typify our characteristic modes of reasoning, that the average person who cares very little for the niceties of dialectic, may and often does, shift his mental gears from the Platonic high to the Aristotelian law and *vice versa* without knowing it." Yes, Coleridge was right in the main. To conclude, Dunning says "A genius peculiarly susceptible to Athenian inspiration must necessarily be in many respects as universal as humanity itself. Such a genius was Aristotle and such was the character of his philosophy."

21

The Political Philosophy of Aristotle

The Political Philosophy of Aristotle cannot be minimised or under estimated. Really he is great in this field. Aristotle was a versatile genius. His knowledge was encyclopaedic and he wrote on ethics and metaphysics, art and poetry, economics and politics, physics and mechanics, physiology and medicine, and astronomy and logic. He has been called "the philosopher" of the ages. He is the father of realism. His chief and most famous work, the 'Politics' is a classical statement of Greek political thought. It is based on a detailed study of a number of governments of his time. It is really a justification of existing institutions like the State, slavery and family or is meant to suggest remedies for the ills of the body-politics of the city-state. Aristotle's political thought is found mainly in this book.

Plato was imaginative and poetic. He reasoned deductively from abstract philosophic conceptions of justice and virtue. But in the words of Gettell, "Aristotle was practical, logical and systematic. He reasoned inductively from a comparative and scientific study of the governmental systems that were actually in existence. His discussions, based on history and observation, are clear and precise with relatively little poetic or allegorical embellishment." His 'Ethics' discusses the nature of individual happiness; in 'Politics', which is intimately connected with his 'Ethics', he treats of the State as one of the chief means through which an individual attains the happiness. The object of Aristotle's 'Politics', is both practical and speculative *i.e.,* to explain the nature of the best state in which the end of happiness may be best realised.

In the words of John Rowle, "Aristotle, besides being a shrewd judge of character and situations is the greatest of early scientists. The 'Politics' is only a small part of his writings, and scientific interests overshadow his ethical and political thought. Aristotle's immensely powerful, classifying, assimilative mind breaks away from the clear-cut geometrical pattern of the 'Republic' and the 'Laws' the 'Politics' is a different and confused book, a quarry of arguments and profound definitions, the thought behind them becoming apparent as the argument proceeds.

The philosophical premises are similar to Plato's, but Aristotle does not argue about them; where Plato is set on constructing a planned State in the light of assumed principles and will often brush aside practical objections, Aristotle is constantly testing his hyphtheses by the facts. There is a sense, in the reading of the 'Politics', of being in touch with a mind of immense power, with enormous reserves; but Aristotle in his work has little consideration of the reader following out his own thought for his own satisfaction without much regard for his audience. Sometimes there seems a staggering callousness and lack of imagination; at others a penetrating insight. The book is the work of a master in intellect, not overtouched with pity, drawing of great erudition.

'The Politics' is an incomplete work. It is a heap of arguments and theories, sometimes repeated or left unfinished. Scholars have expressed almost contradictory opinion about its worth. Besides the above remarks of John Bowle, Dr. Zeller analogises 'the politics' as the richest treasure that has come down to us from antiquity, the greatest contribution to political philosophy that we possess. On the other hand, Dr. Taylor holds that no work of Aristotle is quite so common place in its handling of so vast a subject.

These contradictory remarks about the 'Politics' are because of the fact that it is an unfinished work, containing frequent repetitions, omissions, contradictions, obscurities, inaccuracies and inconsistencies. If at one place reference is made to a topic as it has been discussed earlier without its having been touched at all, at other places references are made to what is discussed at later stages. Sometimes there are abrupt changes in the discussion of topics in the book as a whole. The only probability for these defects is that the 'Politics' as it is, an incomplete book. These works appear to be either notes taken down by his pupils or rough notes prepared by Aristotle himself for lectures delivered at different times and put together in the form of a book at a later date.

It is because of the reason probably Aristotle did not find time to give finishing touches to his took. We do not get here the same polish, form and beauty of Plato's classic, 'the Republic'. However, the achievement of Aristotle is not insignificant. Inspite of the rugged nature of his book its central theme is balance of moderation. Hence, the remark of Catlin that 'after Comfucius, Aristotle is the supreme apostle of common sense and the Golden Mean.' Moreover, the confusion of Aristotle is responsible for opening new chapters in Political Science and giving to politics the character of an independent science. The main theme of Aristotle is to reconcile ideals and actualities. Naturally, this attempt gives us a hazardous picture.

Aristotle's Ethics and Politics are great help to constitution-makers and legislators in providing with rules to construct virtue. The Politics is therefore, not a systematic study of political philosophy but rather a treatise on the art of government. In it Aristotle analyses the evils that were prevalent in the Greek cities and the defects in their political systems, and give practical suggestions as to the best way to avoid threatening dangers. The general nature of his political thought may be inferred from the point of view of the work as a whole and from the rational principles underlying his political advice. What Aristotle wrote on was not so much the Ideal State but the ideals of the State. The sketch of the Ideal State remains unfinished.

The Character of Aristotle's Political Philosophy

Aristotle differs from Plato more in the form and method than in the substance or contents of his political philosophy. Aristotle's theories represent definite clear-cut dogmas, bearing a direct relation to his general scheme of political science. Aristotle is analytical and logical in the treatment of his subject. Instead of using *a priori* method of deducing his ideas from abstract notions of virtue and good, Aristotle used the inductive method of formulating his theories as a result of extensive observation and minute analysis of objective facts. Though essentially a realist philosopher, his realism was not without its traces of idealism.

Aristotle attached very great importance to political sciences which treated of the 'highest good' of man. The highest good of man is the perfect development and rational exercise of all the power in him, which is impossible outside the society and, therefore, outside the state. The good of the individual, therefore, is merged in that of the state which is the subject of political science. Aristotle conceived of political science in a double sense, *i.e.,* (1) as a pure science concerned with the absolute good of man and the perfect state and (2) as a practical science dealing with the constitutional relations of actual men in actual societies.

Aristotle was a practical man of the world and a realist philosopher as shown by his defence of slavery and his denunciation of Plato's communism. It was his realism, with its hard logic, fine analysis, keen observation and a touch of idealism that made his theories and observations of abiding and universal interest. On the other hand, "he was too rich in adaptability, too poor in original fancy, to shine as a star of first magnitude among the creators of new ideals."

22

Plato and Aristotle — Views on State

Plato and Aristotle are the two greatest stars in the universe of political philosophy. The former is known as the first poetic philosopher in the history of political thought. His disciple and successor, Aristotle is the father of political science, according to Dunning. Both are the greatest apostles of the great culture. Almost all the thinkers till the beginning of 20th century dark deep from this rich fountain of knowledge of wisdom.

At the beginning of the human civilisation, Plato stands like a colossus. His fame greatly rests upon his masterpiece, 'The Republic', which is an impressive embodiment of scientific genius and political insight. Dunning calls this work essentially a romance consisting of a series of brilliant metaphysical essays wherein politics has been incidentally discussed. Believing as he does that the ideal is the real, the Ideal State constructed in his 'Republic' is meant to be a type or model for all times and climes. It is to be the criterion by which the existing systems can be estimated and an ideal to be emulated. Plato wants to show what in principle the State ought to be rather than what can be. He wants to give the 'Ideal' of the State, not worrying about the practicability of the 'Ideal'.

Aristotle, on the other hand, is soberer, if less original genius, in the words of Salime. He deals with a vast range of subjects in his works. His political philosophy is empirical and descriptive in comparison with the radical and abstract nature of Plato's philosophy. He has a pragmatic approach and hence, he is concerned with what can be in political science. His central theme is balance and moderation and the reconciliation between ideals and actualities. Hence the remark of Catlin that "after Confucious, Aristotle is the supreme apostle of common sense and the Golden Mean." Prof. Maxey draws out a beautiful distinction between the two philosophers.

Plato is a deductive philosopher. He uses inductive facts only when he accepts the human nature to be weak and frail. He starts with certain assumptions and then deduces conclusions logically from it, brushing aside whatever stands in the way of his arguments. His first assumption is, what we see is simply a shadow of the idea which is the final goal of mankind.

Man should try to achieve that object as far as possible. That ideal can be reached by rational man. Now the question is as to how to develop this ability. For this purpose he advances a system of State education. With the help of education, the individual will be able to perceive the 'Idea of Good'. It will result in the beautification of soul which means the inward eye of the individual that will totally understand the inner light.

After having stated that virtue is knowledge and how to train individuals in order to attain that, Plato comes down to earthly realities. He makes another assumption that all men are not equally competent to receive that education because of natural division of aptitude and ability found in them. According to him, human nature is composed of three psychological characteristics called *reason, spirit* and *appetite.* He assumes that in the philosopher-guardians, reason will dominate, and in the military guardians the spirit will dominate. *i.e.,* works and artisans, will look after the production of material goods essential for the sustenance of man. In this classification of human beings he is primarily concerned with what ought to be. That is why he does not bother about the birth or sex of the guardians. Those who are incompetent even if they are the children of guardians should not be appointed to those posts; and if they are fit for the highest duties of the State, no matter they are women or slaves, should be assigned those jobs.

While discussing about the philosopher-guardians, he finds that often the rules in the actual States are distracted by two institutions called family and property. Hence, in order to realistic philosopher-guardians he does hesitate to sweep clean of both of them. In their place he advocates for common meals State-regulated mating, infanticide etc.

Although during his later writings 'The Statesman' and 'the Laws' he realises the impracticability of his Ideal State as portrayed in 'the Republic' due to frailty of human nature he grudgingly recognises the sovereignty of law. He postulates his second best State in the Laws but he states at many places that there is no need of this State if the philosopher guardians can be made available. The institution called the Nocturnal Council is nothing more than a device to usher the philosopher guardian through the back door. His main problem throughout his writings remains to be the search of a philosopher-guardian or the philosopher-king or Super-man who will guide the State.

But Aristotle's approach is entirely different. Although first he also starts with the construction of his Ideal State like other Greek philosophers, but he abandons his attempt later when he starts discussing the political actualities. He comes to certain conclusions after the analysis of many constitutions, about which there is nothing like the ideal but there are ideals, according to Salime. In his best attainable State, Aristotle has shown that he is a realist dealing with common men and not with super-man or philosopher rulers of Plato. He places the sovereignty in such a state in the hands of the middle class, which ensures greatest stability. But this sovereign class is not to have unlettered authority; it is subject to laws. Unlike the philosopher king of Plato who is above the laws in Aristotle's State there is the sovereignty of law. He does not share Plato's idealism and the latter's hatred existing laws, practices and institutions. His sense of reality and compromise does not allow him to portray an ideal State and that makes his State colourless.

In the words of Wayper "He began this method of observation and of deducing general conclusions from actual practice which has, as it were, anchored political thought to earth. His interest in the 'Politics', his concern with the best good in existing circumstances, his conviction that we must take States as they are and do the best we can with them, his belief that political mechanics, his insistence on the value of the rule of law or disembodied wisdom, his realisation that some constitutions would not grow in certain soils, all played a great part in the development of political thought."

Aristotle also states that the ultimate aim of state is the realisation of good life. But he deals with actual states and tells various methods to maintain them including tyranny. His methods of averting revolutions are not based on ethical or idealistic principles, but on expedience pure and simple as of example, to create imaginary fears to maintain security. In the words of Salime, "Both democracy and oligarchy tend to degenerate into tyranny, which his bad in itself and also unlikely to be successful. The almost cynical freedom with which Aristotle advises the tyrant presages Machiavelli. The traditional tactics are to degrade and humiliate all who might be dangerous, to keep subjects powerless and to create divisions and mistrust among them."

According to Aristotle, moderation is the true key for success. His endeavour has always been to maintain a balance among the conflicting forces. There is nothing like what ought to be in Aristotle but only what can be. He emphasises on climate, geography, social character, customs etc. as the determining factors of State clearly show that we must make the best out of a given situation but should not aspire for an ideal.

In the words of Maxey, "Plato's State is a fabric of abstract ideas to be translated into reality by a philosopher-king who will sweep away all existing institutions and employ genetics and education to create a new and better race of men in a perfect social order. Aristotle's is a fabric of materials already existing, thoroughly tried, well understood, and lying at head ready for use by any intelligent statesman who dares to try his skill at weaving them into patterns approximating the ideal. Yet both thinkers display the same ethical fervour, the same passion for order, the same love for moderation, the same devotion to justice and reason, the same confidence in education, the same faith in humanity, and the same concern for the realisation of good life."

Some critics like Dr. Popper accuse Aristotle because of his practical approach, for vulgarising political science. He says that Aristotle was compelled to be realistic because he had to earn his living by drafting constitutions for innumerable city-states that came up like mushrooms in him times.

Salime compares the two philosophers; "In originality and boldness of speculative construction he was by no means the equal of Plato and the underlying principles of his philosophy were all derived from his master. In the power of intellectual organisation especially in the ability to grasp a pattern, or a tendency in a vast and complicated a mass of details he was not only superior to Plato but the equal of any thinker in the later history of science."

Let us conclude with the remarks of Maxey; "As Plato is father to the idealists, romanticists, revolutionists and utopians of political philosophy, so Aristotle is father to the realists, scientists, pragmatists and utilitarians. All who believe in new worlds for old are disciples of Plato; all who believe in old worlds made new by the tedious and toilsome use of science are disciples of Aristotle."

23

Politics of Aristotle — Some Important Synopsis

Book I

Aristotle in his Book I of Politics has described the views on state in the following manner :

"Every state is a community of some kind and every community is established with a view to some good;.....The state or political community, which is the highest of all, and which embraces all the rest aims, and in a greater degree than any other, at the highest good."

According to Aristotle the state belongs to the genius 'Community'. Like the family or the village it is an association of human beings, and it represent the highest form of human association. Every association or community is formed for the sake of some good. So also the state, the supreme and all embracing entity, must aim at the supreme good. Its end is imminent in itself and that end is the life of reason and moral action.

The state is a community of communities. It exists for the sake of good life. For this he includes two things, *i.e.,* moral and intellectual activities. The highest good of man lies in the perfect development and activity of all the powers, moral and intellectual, that are in him, and this is impossible outside the state. The aim of state is to develop the individuals fully in all respects.

Aristotle means the city-state here every citizen knows every other. Here only a small community can lead on virtuous life.

In Book I he mentions the following thing very crisply and clearly :

"Hence, it is evident that the state is the creation of nature and that man is by nature a political animal."

Here Aristotle stresses the view that the state, like the family or household is not an artificial organisation, but a natural organism. The natural instincts of reproduction and preservation create the natural institution of family. The natural families combine into villages and latter into the natural state.

Aristotle advocates two contemporary Greek views regarding his conception of his state; (1) the view of some of the sophists such as Lycophron or Thracymachus that the law and the state are mere products of convention representing interferences with the liberty of the individual and (2) the view of the Cynics the wise man is sufficient unto himself and should repudiate citizenship of any particular state.

In describing the state particular state as a natural institution, Aristotle does not make it independent of human volition.

Aristotle says that the state is a natural institution, and hence man is by nature a political animal. The man is man, *i.e.*, he is better than a brute, only if he lives in a state. Without the civilising influence of speech and organised association, he would be merely an animal not a rational animal. A man satisfies his moral and spiritual, as also partly his economic cravings only through the medium of the State. One cannot live in association with his fellows or has no need for civil society is, says Aristotle, either a beast or a God. There is a social instinct on all of us as indicated by the faculty of speech, which makes social or political animals. To man alone nature has give the sense to distinguish right and wrong, just and unjust, for nature wanted the individuals to live a civic life.

In Book I of politics Aristotle has given a graphic picture regarding slavery in the following manner :

"For he who can foresee with his mind is by nature intended to be lord and master and he who can work with his body is a subject, and by nature a slave."

While discussing the origin of the state, Aristotle mentions the household which contains the male and the female and the master and the slave. Referring to the household as a natural institution, Aristotle is confronted with the problem of finding a rational justification for slavery. The Sophists before him held the view that slavery was not natural but conventional, that there was no natural distinction between master and slave and that slavery was rooted not in nature but in law and violence and as such was unjust. Aristotle disagrees with the Sophists, regards slavery as essential to the household and defends it as natural and, therefore, moral.

Men differ from each other in their intellectual and physical fitness. There are those whose high endowment of reason fits them to command and direct; there are, on the other side, those whose meagre intellectual equipment fits them only to understand and carry out orders. The former are by nature masters; the latter are by nature slaves.

The combination of the above two is essential to the realisation of those purposes for which the household exists; therefore slavery is in accordance with nature, that is, natural.

Aristotle points out that nature intends some men to be slaves. Some men are by nature superior in intellect and masters and others are by nature inferior and slaves. Aristotle is quite aware that in actual fact some slaves are superior to their masters in intellect but he brushes this fact aside as an accident, generally an accident of war in which very superior men may be captured as prisoners of war and enslaved.

Book III

Regarding governments he mentions the following :

"So a multitude is a better judge of many things than an individual."

The last portion of Book III of the Politics represents a long discussion which Aristotle impartially discusses the merits of the various constitutions.

Aristotle believes that the aggregate virtue and ability of the mass of the people is greater than the virtue and ability of a part of the mass. This leads Aristotle to favour a vague sort of democracy. He would give ultimate sovereign power to the mass of citizens, though the actual reins of government would be in the hands of the best citizens only.

Many ordinary persons may be collectively better than a few good ones. Here Aristotle mixes together wisdom and virtue and relies on the superiority of popular judgment on truth in his contention. It often happens that a scheme devised multitude is focussed on it, to present defects not suspected by its wisest member. Aristotle does not admit the universal applicability of this argument. In any case he is only for allowing some "collective" functions to multitude.

The permanent exclusion of the multitude from all offices is dangerous because it produces widespread discontent.

An individual is likely to be overcome by passion; the multitude are unlikely, all of them, to get into passion at once. Aristotle is here treating the members of the crowd as isolated units and is ignoring the fact that the crowd as isolated units and is ignoring the fact that the crowd is apt to be carried away by the passion of its most passionate members.

Though Aristotle prefers the judgement and, therefore, the claims to rule of the multitude over the individual, he is prepared to assign preference to that individual in the state who transcends and all others not only individually but to the whole mass of them collectively in excellence. But then such men who are above laws and whose monarchy represents the best constitution are seldom to be found.

Thus, Aristotle's Politics has indicated his exemplary views on Political Thought.

Bibliography

1. A.R.M. Murray, *An Introduction to Plitical Philosophy.*
2. C.C. Maxey, *Political Philosphies.*
3. Durant Will, *The Story of Philosophy.*
4. Gomperz, *Greek Thinkers.*
5. R.W. Livingstone, ed. *The Legacy of Greece.*
6. G. Lowes Dickinson, *The Greek View of Life.*
7. C.H. Mcllwain, *The Growth of Political Thought in the West.*
8. F.W. Coker, *Readings in Political Philosophy.*
9. George Catlin, *A History of Political Philosophers.*
10. Jowett trans., *The Politics of Aristotle.*
11. M.B. Foster, *Masters of Political Thought*, Volume I.
12. Aristotle, *W.D. Rose.*
13. E. Barker, *Plato and Aristotle.*
14. P. Doyle, *History of Political Thought.*
15. R.G. Gettell, *History of Political Thought.*
16. G.H. Sabine, *History of Political Thought.*
17. W.A. Dunning, *A History of Political Thought : Ancient and Medieval.*
18. W.W. Willoughly, *The Political Theories of the Ancient World.*
19. G.L. Myres, *The Political Ideas of the Greeks.*
20. W. Eberstain, *An Introduction to Political Philosophy.*
21. W. Ebenstein, *Political Thought is Perspective.*
22. Newman, *The Politics of Aristotle.*
23. Richard Mckeon, *Interoduction to Aristotle.*
24. A.E. Taylor, *Aristotle.*
25. A.C. Bradley, Aristotle's Conception of the State.
26. Bhandari and Sethi, *Plato and Aristotle.*
27. J.P. Mayer, *Political Thought : European Traditions.*
28. A.E. Zimmern, *The Greek Commonwealth.*

Index